The Art of
ROMANCE
WRITING

PRACTICAL ADVICE FROM AN
INTERNATIONAL
BESTSELLING ROMANCE WRITER

Valerie Parv

ALLEN&UNWIN

Allen & Unwin
83 Alexander Street
Crows Nest NSW 2065
Australia
Phone: (61 2) 8425 0100
Fax: (61 2) 9906 2218
Email: info@allenandunwin.com
Web: www.allenandunwin.com

National Library of Australia
Cataloguing-in-Publication entry:

Parv, Valerie.
    The art of romance writing.

    2nd ed.
    Bibliography.
    Includes index.
    ISBN 1 74114 374 8

    1. Love stories – Authorship. 2. Fiction – Authorship. I.
    Title.

808.385

Typeset in 11.5/13.5 pt Granjon by Midland Typesetters, Maryborough
Printed by Griffin Press, South Australia

Illustration: Paul Parv; Plot chart p. 141.

10 9 8 7 6 5 4 3 2 1

*f*or my husband, Paul,
with love,
and for all the writers who tell me
this is their favourite book on writing.
I wish you every success.

Contents

Preface

Depression and squalor are for those under twenty-five, they can take it, they even like it, they still have enough time left. But real life is bad for you, hold it in your hand long enough, and you'll get pimples and become feeble-minded. You'll go blind.

Margaret Atwood, 'What is a woman's novel',
Portfolio, December 1986

*T*his quote appeared in the first edition of *The Art of Romance Writing* and it remains one of the most eloquent defences of the romance novel I have read, even if Margaret Atwood didn't have this purpose in mind when she wrote it. Too much real life *is* bad for you. Everyone needs an escape, a safety valve, where dreams and fantasies can be indulged before we return to the fray.

Romance novels have been fulfilling this purpose since the time of Jane Austen and Samuel Richardson. As the world grows increasingly turbulent, we need an escape from reality more than ever. As well, romances can be the modern purveyors of our ancient myths and legends, making their role an important one indeed.

The publishers of romances still provide the most accessible market for a new novelist. Not that this translates as easy; far from it. Above all, your book must be a great read that keeps the editor turning pages. Every editor says they're looking for a terrific book. Although different editors have different definitions of what this means, the book must first excite *you*, before it can appeal to anyone else.

John Boon, grandson of the founder of Mills & Boon, says the London office alone receives between 4000 and 5000 manuscripts a year, and accepts perhaps ten or twelve. Thankfully, I didn't know this when I started out and was fortunate to be accepted on my first submission. Even so, this acceptance took a year and launched me on a learning curve which continues today, after publishing around 60 romances and twenty non-fiction books. One of the fascinations of romance writing is that it has so many facets that one can never fully master them all.

When I started writing romances, there was almost no practical information available to new writers. Most learning was of the 'hands-on' variety and, most painful of all, trial and error. In an attempt to help other writers short-cut this stage, I wrote the first edition of *The Art of Romance Writing*. Since then, the popularity of romance novels has grown around the world, and the genre now encompasses a variety of sub-genres such as chick lit, inspirationals, romantic comedy and erotica. All of these sub-genres provide new and exciting markets for would-be romance writers, and each demands a careful study of their specialised requirements before submission.

With a readership of millions around the world, romance writing is worthy of your best efforts. More than the much-vaunted financial gains to be made is the satisfaction of knowing that readers in countries as far apart as Iceland, Turkey, Japan, Korea, Russia and Brazil are reading your words, learning a little about your favourite backgrounds and sharing your treasured fantasies.

It may encourage you to know that you're in excellent company. Mills & Boon didn't start publishing romances until the 1930s. Its stable of authors reads like a 'who's who' of the writing profession. Hugh Walpole and P.G. Wodehouse, Jack London, Georgette Heyer, Sir Arthur Conan Doyle and Rosamund Pilcher (of *The Shell Seekers* fame) were all published by Mills & Boon. One of its first works was the English translation of Gaston Leroux's *Phantom of the Opera*.

I recommend using this list as inspiration when the going becomes hard—as it always does at some point. Every writer suffers from insecurity, fear of failure, writer's block and a myriad of other frustrating conditions. We write in spite of them. I was once asked, 'How do you know when you start writing that you can do it?' The answer is that you start writing to find out *if* you can do it. There's no other way.

In the creation of this edition I owe thanks to a great many people, certainly too many to mention individually. Paul, Leigh, Des and Margie, your support is still appreciated a decade on. My students at various writing courses over the years have taught me as much as I have taught them. My editors have further rounded out my literary education, starting with the legendary Jacqui Bianchi; and my agent/manager, Linda Tate, continues to be a tower of strength on my creative journey.

Also, thank you to my fellow romance writers in Australia and around the world for generously letting me quote from your books and your experiences; to all at Harlequin Mills & Boon and Silhouette for your support; to the members of the romance writing organisations mentioned in these pages—new writers can do yourselves no greater favour than to join one or more of them for encouragement, support and professional development; to the published and aspiring members of eHarlequin.com, especially those in the dark reaches of the Bat Cave; and to Patrick Gallagher and the team at Allen & Unwin, notably Alex Nahlous and Annette Barlow, this book's godmother twice over.

Valerie Parv
Canberra 2004

1
Why romance?

'**My** daughter wants to write romantic fiction,' said the voice on the phone. 'Can you tell me the formula so I can pass it on to her?'

I've been asked this often enough to wish that there *was* a formula I could give them. It would be easier than trying to explain that romance novels of the type published by Harlequin, Mills & Boon and Silhouette are not as easy to write as they are to read. There is no recipe which will guarantee fame and fortune. The so-called formula is merely a set of conventions which differentiate romance from, say, thrillers or detective novels. Within the conventions, detailed in this book, you can write your own story. In fact, publishers urge you to write the book you would enjoy reading, rather than slavishly imitating what's already on the market.

It's a lot like baking a cake. Just as a number of cooks may start with the same ingredients and all produce different results, you can take the basic ingredients for a romance novel and work them into an original story. The reader may know from the beginning that the characters will live happily ever after but you should make them worry that maybe, this time, they won't get together. The course of true love certainly should not run smoothly—as in predictably—from beginning to end. In many contemporary romances, particularly the longer single-title novels, it's often sufficient to provide a satisfactory resolution,

2 ♥ *The Art of Romance Writing*

rather than a true happy-ever-after. Marriage proposals are far from a necessity. In the chick lit sub-genre, editors talk about Mr Right for Now, rather than Mr Right.

Romances are not all alike any more than spy stories, westerns or science fiction novels are all alike. They are grouped together because they offer the reader certain common elements; hence the description *genre* fiction, meaning fiction of a certain kind.

American author Jayne Ann Krentz says,

> At the core of each genre lie a group of ancient myths unique to that genre. The most popular writers in those genres continue to mine those ancient myths and legends for the elements that make their particular genre work. Westerns and mysteries incorporate the old chivalric tales. The horror genre relies on the gut-wrenching myths of the supernatural that have been around since the days when people lived in caves. Science fiction uses the myths of exploration and fear of the 'other' that have long fascinated an aggressive species bent on conquering new territory. At the heart of the romance novel lie the ancient myths that deal with the subject of male–female bonding.
>
> Stories become myths because they embody values that are crucially important to the survival of the species. There is no subject more imperative to that survival than the creation of a successful pair bond. The romance novel captures the sense of importance and the sheer excitement of that elemental relationship as no other genre can.

We don't expect our romances to work out as well in real life as they do in novels, any more than fans of crime fiction expect every crime to be solved. We read romances, as Krentz says, to reinforce the goals and values associated with our survival as a species.

This closeness to our history may explain why romance novels are so often denigrated. All of us, male and female, want to be loved and appreciated by someone special. It may be such a deep need that we trivialise it rather than admit how important it really is to us.

Lofty ideals? Perhaps. But surely there are more rational explanations for the worldwide popularity of romance novels than the usual one of escapist entertainment. Entertainment value alone hardly explains why almost half of all the paperbacks sold today are romances. According to one editor, an Australian paperback novel can expect to sell between 3000 and 5000 copies. Romance publishers traditionally pay low royalties (between 4 and 6 per cent of the cover price) but worldwide sales can number in the millions.

Who reads romance fiction?

More than 200 million women a year read Harlequin books. This is ten times more than the entire population of Australia. It's a market which boggles the imagination.

It's a common misconception that romance readers belong to one age group or socioeconomic background. Harlequin's research shows that women of all ages read romances, and that half of them are aged between 25 and 44. A third are employed full time; 22 per cent are single and working; a third are housewives; and the rest are students and retired people. In other words, romances are read by women of all ages and backgrounds. Many are well educated with high family incomes. Twenty per cent read a book a day and 40 per cent read a romance novel every two days. Australian author Dorothy Cork credits the women's liberation movement with helping to bring romance reading 'out of the closet'. These days, readers don't care if they are seen reading *Surrender in Paradise* rather than *Paradise Lost*. As another writer observed, there's no safer sex than a romance novel.

With such a discerning readership, you can't afford to be cynical or tongue-in-cheek in your approach. A Silhouette editor points out that those who read and enjoy romance novels often make the best writers. I would go further and say that if you can't find genuine enjoyment in reading romance novels, you will have a hard time writing them at all. I still read several new titles every month to keep up with trends.

These days there's a vast choice of sub-genres, single-title novels and imprints known as 'lines' (branded ranges of books such as Silhouette Desire or Harlequin Intrigue) catering to different readerships. Read a variety of books until you find one you feel comfortable with. This is probably the kind of book you should initially try writing.

While reading, look for differences such as the level of sensuality, whether the background is exotic or only mentioned in passing, how many viewpoint characters are used, and whether the focus is entirely on the romance or includes other story elements. I suggest you read each book twice, once for entertainment and again to analyse structure and content. What are the ages and occupations of the characters? Are there any suspense or mystery elements? Do the characters make love or does the action stop at the bedroom door?

You can learn a great deal from the books you dislike. Which parts bored you? Why? Was the story predictable? How might the author have avoided the problem? Did the characters irritate you? If you were the author, how would you have handled the characters to avoid irritation?

Analysing the books you don't like can be as fruitful as

studying those you do enjoy. When you find an imprint you like, check inside for the publisher's name and address, usually located after the title page. Write or email the editor of your chosen imprint and request the publisher's writers' guidelines—also called tip sheets, particularly in the United States. An example of a tip sheet is included as Appendix I to give you an idea of what to expect. The tip sheet usually sets out basic requirements such as length, acceptable backgrounds, preferred age range of hero and heroine, desirable viewpoints, use of secondary characters and subplots, and the level of sexual involvement between the main characters.

Some publishers leave such choices up to the author, and others spell out whether the characters may have sex before marriage. Incidentally, the traditional 'marriage of convenience' plotline, in which the hero and heroine marry for practical reasons and gradually fall in love with each other, which appears in so many older romance novels, was often a way of allowing the characters to make love within the moral framework of the time. It is still used to this end where sex before marriage is unpopular with a certain readership. The publishers don't make these rules lightly. They have usually done their market research and established what their readers want, so it's better to write for an imprint which suits your personal style than to expect it to change to accommodate the book you want to write.

Can men write romances?

Men can and do write romances successfully, although usually under a female pseudonym so their work isn't pre-judged on the basis of their gender. Men also suffer from discrimination, sometimes.

One of the best-known male writers was the late Tom Huff, who wrote as Jennifer Wilde. Several married couples share pen-names, giving a nice balance of male and female viewpoint within their books. For a man to write romance successfully, he has to train himself to think and feel from a woman's point of view. Editors say that male writers tend to use harsher vocabulary—words like pushing, pulling and tugging—in their love scenes; a woman might write of stroking, caressing and enfolding. A male writer must be able to focus on the woman's feelings during a love scene.

For example, few women think of their breasts as their most attractive feature yet a male writer may have the heroine think about 'her beautiful breasts' during a love scene, taking the reader out of the heroine's viewpoint.

Not only male writers make this mistake. In my early books, I used to write about what 'they' were doing, taking the all-seeing, godlike point of view rather than focusing on what my heroine was thinking and feeling at that moment. Now I write 'she' instead of 'they'. The chapter on viewpoint explores this important technique in more detail.

Mike Hinkemeyer writes suspense novels under his own name and romance novels as Vanessa Royale. He says he tends to dwell on the darker side of human nature, while his alter ego, Vanessa, is more trusting. Mike says he is the sort of red-blooded male who would appeal to Vanessa.

A useful book for exploring female sexuality is *Women, Sex and Pornography* by Beatrice Faust. This Australian study shows in academic terms how women's view of sexuality differs from men's. In a chapter entitled 'King Kong had XY chromosomes', Faust compares the body traits which men *imagine* that women admire with those they really do admire. Twenty-one per cent of men in her study said that a muscular chest and shoulders was most admired. Only 1 per cent of women chose this body feature, while 39 per cent chose a man's buttocks, specifically when they were described as small and sexy.

Beatrice Faust says that a woman watching a sexy movie tends to imagine what it would be like to change places with the woman in it, even changing the story a little so it meshes with her own life and becomes more credible. She might also feel she is learning lessons she can put into practice in her own romantic life. A man, on the other hand, 'objectifies. He takes the girl down off the screen and has sex with her on the spot'. The danger for male romance writers is clear. While male viewpoint is generally welcome, you must avoid putting yourself exclusively in the hero's place. You are writing for a largely female readership who want to vicariously fall in love with the hero.

Among many other useful books which can help both male and female writers to create strong, believable characters are *The Psychology of Romantic Love* by Nathaniel Branden, *Why Men Are the Way They Are* by Warren Farrell and any of the *Men are from Mars, Women are from Venus* series by John Gray. I am endlessly intrigued by the different ways in which men and women view the world. There's no need to fear running out of story material.

According to former film producer, teacher and broadcasting manager, Valerie Gray, now editor of MIRA Books:

> The interesting thing about romance fiction is that the number of sub-genres is growing by leaps and bounds. Chick lit, kick-ass women, inspirational, romantic fantasy, paranormal are some examples of the kinds of interests our

readers have—and we are responding to that. I think we will continue to see books that feature strong, independent women who lead interesting lives, and by interesting, I don't mean that they are super-rich or super-gorgeous or super-lucky. Mostly our heroines are people just like you and me—ordinary people who are capable of extraordinary things.

Chick lit

So what are these sub-genres that are growing 'by leaps and bounds'? The most radical is the sub-genre dubbed 'chick lit', shorthand for chick literature, because it is primarily read by young women in their 20s and 30s.

Inspired by the 1996 bestselling novel *Bridget Jones's Diary* (Fielding), the chick lit sub-genre is 'setting the pace for an otherwise struggling fiction industry', according to American ABC news journalist, Heather Cabot. 'In the $23 billion US publishing industry, chick lit books earned publishers more than $71 million in 2002.'

Initially, the books followed the Bridget Jones pattern of single women working their way through the modern minefield of careers and personal relationships with varying degrees of success. Readers typically say they enjoy the books because they reflect the reality of their everyday lives. Now chick lit itself is fragmenting into 'mummy lit' and 'baby lit' where the characters explore themes like motherhood and parenting, while still maintaining the true-to-life narratives and humour of the originals. Former publisher and manuscript assessor Brian Cook added 'biz chick lit' to the list, which he describes as chick lit set in a high-powered business environment.

Chick lit and its derivatives are not simply category

romances featuring a 20-something heroine and lots of brand name-dropping. The sub-genre has its own distinctive language and characteristics reflecting the lives and times of its readers. Most are written in the first person, although this is not a requirement. The language must be intelligent and witty, with plenty of self-deprecating humour. Also, the grammar police have to learn to relax and enjoy the creative use of language and the capitalisation of everyday nouns, turning them into labels such as Helen Fielding's Smug Marrieds in *Bridget Jones's Diary*. These narrative touches help to differentiate chick lit from more traditional forms of romance.

But make no mistake, they are still romances. Bridget and her counterparts are still looking for Mr Right, even if life forces them to settle for Mr Right for Now. And Bridget Jones in her turn is a modern incarnation of Jane Austen's Elizabeth in *Pride and Prejudice*.

As Zareen Jaffrey, editorial assistant for chick lit line Red Dress Ink, points out, you still need to write a novel all your own. Publishers want distinctive voices, not clones of Helen Fielding. You need to create a heroine with real-life problems, and show readers how she works through them. Dating may not be her whole concern. She may well be married with a career and even children, provided she is on a journey to her future that readers can share.

Readers should recognise themselves and their lives in your character's personal qualities and life concerns. The story will be complex and the ending unpredictable. That's probably the main difference between chick lit and traditional romances. The men and the roadblocks you place in the heroine's way should keep editor and reader guessing as to how it will all work out—or even *if* it will.

A further development from chick lit is the 'kick-ass'

heroine and storylines found in lines such as Silhouette's Bombshell. These are female action–adventure novels of 80 000 to 90 000 words in which a strong, savvy heroine saves the day.

The heroine may find herself in dangerous, often high-stakes situations and has the ability to get herself and others out of trouble by using her own skills. While the books contain romantic subplots and the heroine does get her man in the end, the romance is secondary to the action–adventure elements. The conclusion needs to be satisfactory and 'take the relationship to the next level' but does not necessarily end in marriage. Like chick lit, the action–adventure romance has evolved to reflect the needs and concerns of contemporary readers for whom marriage is an ideal, but not necessarily attainable or sustainable.

Rosie Koop, Publishing Manager of Harlequin in Australia, says that it's important for chick lit and kick-ass books to have 'the wow factor', an attention-grabbing concept which is both original and provocative. Characters should be empathetic and engaging, and the situations you place your heroine in must resonate with the reader as reflective of their life. Publishers seeking chick lit submissions include Red Dress Ink, New American Library (NAL), Kensington Publishing Group, Pocket Books and Random House Australia.

Romantic comedy

This has been emerging as a sub-genre over the last few years with mainstream publishers such as St. Martin's Press and lines like Harlequin's Duet line, and its successor, Flipside. Inspired by the success of television shows and movies like *My Big Fat Greek Wedding*, *Will and Grace* and *Friends*, romantic comedy novels place fun and likable characters in real-life dilemmas, while still maintaining a fairly traditional romantic core.

The difference is in your handling of the narrative. The mood is usually fast-paced, with little in the way of introspection. There is room for writers to develop non-traditional plots and secondary characters provided they complement the central romance.

While specialised lines may be devoted exclusively to romantic comedy, it can also be found within more traditional lines. Harlequin have created a subcategory called Tango, as a home for category-length romances featuring less traditional elements such as humour. An example is Liz Fielding's *City Girl in Training*. In mainstream fiction, authors such as Jennifer Crusie have made a specialty out of romantic comedy with titles like *Faking It*, described on the cover as 'bright, funny, sexy and wise', and Stephanie Bond's *Our Husband*, also described as 'fresh, funny and sexy', has the characteristic elements of romantic comedy.

Paranormal romances

According to Romance Writers of America, these are 'romances containing other-worldly elements such as magic, mystic characters or fantasy and science fiction elements'. Time-travel books, where characters travel between past and present or present and future, are also included in this sub-genre. An example is Merline Lovelace's *Somewhere in Time*. In this book, an air force pilot brings her jet down in a bizarre windstorm and finds herself living in Roman times two thousand years in the past and falling for Lucius, senior centurion of the Roman Empire.

Author Kristin Hannah says, 'The future of these books is as unlimited as the future of romance itself. Our readers love epic fantasies, dark Gothics with a supernatural twist, time travels, futuristics. The more of these that are written and published, the greater the demand.'

As with all sub-genres, you should only write them because you enjoy their special challenges and requirements, rather than trying to fit market trends. Reading widely in the areas that interest you is the best way to start. Identify the conventions that make paranormals work. How do the authors make magic believable, for example? In a time-travel book, how long does the time-shifted character spend adjusting to the change before getting on with the story? How is the time shift achieved to make it convincing? How is the romance resolved to everyone's satisfaction? Even time travel and magic require rules and, once established, they must be consistent.

Your paranormal elements must be integral to the plot, and should not be able to be removed without damaging the story. In Nora Roberts's series *The Donovan Legacy*, the books would not have worked if the lead characters had not been witches or, as she termed it, had elvan blood. Imagine J.R.R. Tolkien's *Lord of the Rings* being set anywhere but Middle Earth? Or Anne Rice's books without the vampire elements. You aren't writing an ordinary tale where the characters just happen to be vampires or time travellers. The paranormal elements must enhance and enrich the story.

Single-title romances

According to single-title and Superromance author Brenda Novak, the main difference between single-title novels and romances written for a particular line is reader expectation.

Lines have traditionally indicated the kind of experience the reader can expect. Thus a book flagged 'sweet' can be assumed to contain very little explicit sex or pre-marital lovemaking. Single-title romances are not so readily defined. Each book stands alone on its own merits. As Rosie Koop says, 'The brand name is the author.'

Marketing of single-titles is also approached differently. The books are more likely to be issued in trade paperback size, may be promoted more extensively by publishers, and tend to stay on bookstore shelves longer than the average one-month shelf life of category romance novels.

Single-title books, sometimes grouped together as 'women's fiction', retain romance as a central element, but will also contain subplots and well-developed secondary characters. Says Koop, 'The depth and complexity must be larger.' However, the differences between category romances and single-titles is narrowing all the time.

Short romances range from 50 000 words to 85 000, whereas single-titles start from 90 000 to 150 000. This gives you room to explore more complex themes and subplots, and to experiment with more detailed settings and edgier storylines.

However, it's not a good idea to take your rejected category novel and try to 'stretch' it to fit a longer line. Adding subplots for the sake of them can make the story confusing. The subplot should be integral to the main story, demonstrating different aspects of the main characters, or otherwise adding depth (not just length) to the story.

Secondary characters should also enhance the main action, adding complexity and interest to make the story more interesting.

Single-titles can encapsulate everything from historical

romances like those written by *New York Times* bestselling author, Stephanie Laurens, to quirky contemporaries in the Jennifer Crusie mould. There is also room for multicultural themes, romantic comedy and fantasy/paranormal elements. In a recent Harlequin acquisition, the hero is a statue come to life, Koop says.

Most of the publishers listed in this book are open to submissions for single-title romances. In the case of Harlequin's HQN line debuting in late 2004, no agent is required and authors are invited to submit a synopsis and three sample chapters, as specified in the writers' guidelines available from Harlequin or on the web.

Erotica

Years ago I taught a workshop on romance writing at Sancta Sophia College, Sydney University. Apart from an interesting juxtaposition of subject and venue, I was intrigued to hear one of the other tutors tell students that in a romance novel 'you don't even get to kiss the horse'.

Aside from why the heroine would want to kiss a horse when there's a hunky hero on hand, this statement reflects a basic misconception that, until recently, romance heroines have all been chaste and virginal.

This hasn't been true for the whole twenty or more years I've been writing and studying the field. Romance writers have been pushing the envelope of what's permissible at about the same rate that society has been doing so. My earliest romance novels encapsulated premarital sex, abused wives, war neurosis and adoption issues, so they are far from new elements.

These days, depending on the line you're writing for, there are almost no taboos or language that can't be used somewhere within the vast panoply of romance fiction. Naturally, if you're writing a sweet romance, your characters must meet reader expectations of language and morality. Premarital sex is rarely an option, although the characters no longer need to be virgins. Rather, as Harlequin once phrased it, the question simply need not arise.

At the other end of the spectrum is erotica, such as Harlequin's Blaze line, and books published by Ellora's Cave. The latter defines their books as Romantica, a trademarked term meaning 'any work of literature that is both romantic and sexually explicit. Within this genre, a man and a woman develop "in love" feelings for one another that culminate in a monogamous relationship.'

Up to this point, there is little difference between traditional romance fiction and erotica. However, true erotica, even Romantica, is likely to be expressed in more earthy and frank language, and the characters' sexual experiences are likely to be more adventurous than your average category novel.

Some taboos still remain, however. Most publishers of erotica will not consider books dealing with paedophilia, crude descriptions of bodily functions, and practices that most reasonable adults are likely to consider perverse. This is the main point of difference between erotica and true pornography which has almost none of these limitations. Ellora's Cave also says it will not consider strict erotica without romance.

Inspirational romances

Called 'romance without the blush' on the Spacecoast Authors of Romance website, www.authorsofromance.

com/inspirational.htm, these novels reflect nondenominational Christian values and beliefs.

Romance Writers of America defines inspirational romances as 'a romance novel with religious faith as a significant element of the story'. Publishers include Steeple Hill Books, Barbour Publishing, Harvest House, Tyndale House, Warner Faith and Zondervan. Details of these and other publishers of inspirational romance can be found in the chapter, 'To Market, To Market'.

According to Kelly Edens, writing on the Spacecoast Authors' website, the best writers do not preach their beliefs. In fact, most publishers' guidelines specify that stories should reflect Christian values 'without preaching'. Characters do not have to be perfect although they will rise above their flaws as a result of their beliefs and the lasting love that the hero and heroine find in each other.

With Christian publishing houses committing more and more resources to fiction publishing, the outlook for this sub-genre is promising. Steeple Hill's Joan Marlow Golan says that since 1995 sales in the Christian fiction market have doubled, making it one of the fastest-growing categories in publishing today.

In 2003 Steeple Hill increased the number of short romances it publishes from three to four per month, and branched out into bigger trade paperback novels in a range of sub-genres from suspense and mystery to 'Christian chick lit'.

Publishers from Warner Faith to Zondervan say they are looking for more mainstream submissions in the range of 65 000 to 150 000 words. Descriptions such as 'edgier', 'high concept' and 'character-driven' are being used by editors to describe the kind of novels they'd like to see within the constraints of these burgeoning lines.

Mastering the art

Many aspiring romance writers believe that writing a romance is easy: simply follow the traditional format, employ a pleasant writing style and you're there. One writer told me that she was going to write a romance 'as soon as she had mastered the art of writing in short sentences with a reduced vocabulary'. What Harlequin's tip sheet calls, 'a book that simply makes the right noises' is readily obvious to editors and readers.

What Harlequin and other romance publishers *do* want are:

> . . . romances with a spark of originality, imagination, a freshness of approach and strong, believable characters— not stereotypes . . . stories that centre on the development of the romance between the hero and heroine, with the emphasis on the feelings and emotions of both.
>
> Storylines should be complex enough to maintain interest for the required 50 000 to 100 000-plus words. Depending on the line, subplots may add elements of mystery, suspense and adventure provided the emphasis remains on the central romance.

How to achieve this fine balance will be explored in this book. By the time you have worked through it, you should have chosen the sub-genre best suited to your preferences and writing style, developed a workable synopsis, and be ready to start writing the manuscript, or be able to assess whether the romance novel you have already written is ready for submission. You shouldn't underestimate the value of this preparatory stage. I find that problems not solved in the development stage will loom much larger in the actual writing. Sometimes, the whole book will fall down because a crucial plot, motivation or character point hasn't been solved in the planning stages.

I'm frequently asked where I get my ideas. To a writer, the ideas are the easy part. We pluck them from the air around us. The hard work comes in the writing. Here, I offer you a friendly word of warning: There is nothing quite as seductive as the next idea. An idea which looks fresh and exciting when you first conceive it can lose its lustre when the hard work of writing begins. That's when other ideas begin to beckon like siren songs out of the ether. 'Leave that, write me,' they say. The answer is to jot them down and file them away, then return to the work in hand. There is nothing so vital to a new writer as finishing what you start. Whether the book succeeds or not, you have written a novel. You know you can do it. It is no longer something you are going to do 'some day', along with half the population of the known universe. It is something you have done, and nothing beats the feeling of accomplishment which it brings. Sometimes, a first novel can be reworked as your experience grows, to be published as your third or fourth book.

Submitting your manuscript

All professional writers know the value of allowing a piece of writing to 'cool off' before submission. After a few days or a week away from it, you become more objective in your assessment and more able to spot any flaws. For this reason, I suggest that you allow at least a couple of weeks between completing your manuscript and sending it to a publisher. If you have already completed a book, the checklists can be used to assess whether it is on target before submission, to ensure that you've given your work every chance of acceptance. After evaluating your manuscript with the help of one of the checklists, you may find that it still needs work in one or more areas. Solving these problems at the planning stage will make the writing easier and more likely to appeal to a romance editor when the manuscript is finally submitted.

There are two final points I would like to get out of the way. Publishers usually specify the length of manuscript they require. However difficult it may seem, and no matter how many good reasons you may have, I urge you not to submit work which is appreciably longer or shorter than specified. (A couple of hundred words either way is usually acceptable.) It is the mark of the amateur to plead that the work couldn't possibly be shortened. Reader's Digest managed to publish the Bible as a condensed book. However painful it may be, make the effort to cut out every unnecessary word or phrase. Sometimes, whole characters and subplots have to go for the book to have the correct length and balance, with the emphasis squarely on the developing romance.

The second caution is one which worries many writers much more than it should. What if someone steals your ideas? Within a particular genre, similarities are bound to occur between books. In fact, there is no copyright on ideas, only on the form in which they are presented. No two authors will treat the same theme in exactly the same way. Therefore, you needn't worry that a publisher will steal your idea. Editors are much too busy to bother. It is far easier for them to assign the book to you if they like the idea.

To prove that coincidences do occur, there's the example of my book *The Leopard Tree*, in which the heroine, a UFO enthusiast, meets the hero soon after she sees her first UFO. Is he as human as he appears? No sooner had I submitted the manuscript to Silhouette Books, which later published it, than *Romantic Times* magazine reviewed an American novel describing—you guessed it—a hero who just might have arrived by UFO.

I doubt whether an idea exists which some writer hasn't thought about and possibly discarded. Then along comes another writer with a fresh slant on the same subject and, hey presto, a bestseller. It is your handling of the idea, not the idea itself, which makes it unique. How many times have you read Cinderella in another guise? Or Beauty and the Beast? All the possible variations on these two themes alone could fill a library—and they're far from exhausted yet.

One area you may want to treat with caution is the Internet. Some publishers regard work that has appeared on the Internet as already published, affecting the rights you may be able to sell in future. As well, work appearing on the Internet may not always be protected by copyright conventions, or you may be giving away ownership to the owner of the website without meaning to do so. Before posting your manuscript or work-in-progress on the Internet, it's a good idea to read the fine print at the site, so you know exactly what you're getting into.

Emulating writers you admire is a useful way to get started but you must work towards developing your own unique way of telling a story, your own style, adapted to the special demands of the romance genre.

Remember, there are no hard and fast rules for how to write. What works for one writer may not work for another. What matters is the result.

2
Sense and sensuality

What makes a romance romantic? This is one of the toughest questions to answer but it cannot be ignored. Within the requirements of the genre, you must provide the reader with a full sensory experience—hence the word 'sensuality' in the title of this chapter. Sensual means 'of the senses'. It does not automatically mean sexy, although when the reader's senses are engaged this is often the result.

Regency writer Nancy Richard-Akers (1988) said romance is too often equated only with sexual tension and love scenes. Any scene can be romantic if the reader is drawn to care about the characters and share their experiences vicariously.

Harlequin contends that it isn't enough to write a novel which makes 'the right noises'. As Richard-Akers said, the most important ingredient is the emotional boost provided for the reader through 'living [the characters'] experiences with them and through their eyes'.

If you subscribe to Jayne Ann Krentz's theory that romances are contemporary versions of ancient myths and legends, then romance speaks to the very human need in all of us to love and be loved by someone special. We want to be swept away by the *idea*, if not the reality.

The implicit message is that love is always possible. And who's to say it isn't? A retired man, widowed for more than twenty years, travelled halfway around the world to meet the lady of his dreams. Like him, she was English, but they would never have met if they hadn't decided, quite unbeknown to each other, to take a last-fling trip to Australia. A plot worthy of a romance novel, perhaps, but it really happened to my aunt and uncle.

So your first and most important task is to reinforce the message that love is possible at any age, in any occupation and in the face of any obstacle. This message is delivered throughout your manuscript in various ways, the main ones being characterisation, setting and plot.

People and places

Many writers are surprised to find that setting is not the most important element. They think that setting a story on a tropical island or in the Bahamas will automatically make it romantic. I have set books on the Great Barrier Reef and in my own idyllic invented kingdom of Carramer, but some of my most powerful stories are set against everyday backgrounds. *The Love Artist* was set in a department store. *Remember Me, My Love* revolved around an industrial estate. When the heroine first sees the hero, she is working on an assembly line. *Booties and the Beast* is set in Canberra. Yet these books have all sold well. People are always more important to a reader than places and things. We all yearn to live inside another's skin, alleviating for a while the loneliness of being human.

This doesn't mean that the background need be sketchy or dull. Research shows that readers enjoy learning something about a particular place or profession. The secret is to blend in the details skilfully, a little at a time, like seasoning, so that at no time does the background overshadow the developing romance between your hero and heroine. A good example is the classic *Gone With the Wind* (Mitchell). If you haven't read it for a long time, study it through a writer's eyes. First you'll be surprised to find that it is written almost entirely from Scarlett's viewpoint. Despite the great length of the book, we only deviate from her viewpoint briefly, mainly for the Civil War scenes in which she didn't participate. It is an excellent example of how background should enhance a story rather than dominate it.

Travel is a far more everyday activity now than it was even a couple of decades ago. So readers aren't as likely to buy a romance novel to enjoy vicariously an exotic locale they may never get a chance to see. Instead, they are looking for a gripping story about two people defying almost insurmountable odds to live 'happily ever after', with the setting, careers of the protagonists and other background details adding colour and excitement to the story.

Silhouette editor Lucia Macro says she enjoys romances 'brimming with electricity'. She is irritated by conflicts which are caused by outside forces—the 'Other Woman', for example—and prefers to see the conflict arise from within the relationship, from the characters of the hero and heroine.

To cite *The Love Artist* again: Carrie Doyle is the daughter of an artist who left his family high and dry to pursue his art. She is determined not to suffer, as her mother did, by falling in love with a ne'er-do-well artist. When she finds herself strongly attracted to a professional cartoonist, she must struggle with her desires, trying to decide whether to follow her head or her heart.

In *Romance Writers Report*, the journal of the Romance Writers of America, Lucia Macro urges writers not to have the hero and heroine declare their love for each other before the end of the story:

> No matter what the heroine admits, the hero should remain close-mouthed about his feelings until the very end. By having him speak too soon, you destroy your romantic tension.

She says she sees too many books where the hero declares his love and proposes halfway through the book. 'The remainder of the story is spent with the heroine making excuses not to accept his marriage proposal.'

The fantastic hero

Most editors agree that the single element which makes a romance truly romantic is a fantastic hero. As editor Anne Gisonny suggests, it isn't enough for the heroine to fall in love with the hero; the reader has to fall in love with him, too.

'Part of what makes these books romantic,' says Lucia Macro, 'is the intensity of the emotions we see—and the intensity of emotions we *feel*—with regard to the love story. Sensuality is certainly responsible in part for this.'

How do you make the reader feel what your characters feel? A key element is *sexual tension*—the heart of every successful romance novel. Without it, you may have an enjoyable novel, but you won't have a romance.

So what is sexual tension and how do you create it?

Sexual tension is recognisable as much by what doesn't happen between the characters as by what does. All the ingredients can be there, the characters touching, looking into each other's eyes, yet—nothing. The tension is lost because the writer fails to involve the reader so totally in the scene that they see, hear, feel, even smell, all that the heroine does, vicariously experiencing the heroine's reactions to the hero and what they mean to her.

In real life, as Macro points out, if you looked into a man's eyes at a party and felt a flutter in your stomach, you'd probably decide you were hungry and head for the buffet. But that's real life. Romance has to sound real while being larger than life, involving all the reader's senses to the full.

Susan Napier creates wonderful sexual tension in her Harlequin Mills & Boon romance *Another Time*. This passage is just one of many examples of how the heroine's heightened sensitivity to the hero is shared with the reader, sensation by sensation:

> A bee buzzed between them, its sultry hum filling the silence. Helen studied it with the dedication of an entomologist. Unfortunately the wretched insect chose to settle on Alex's naked chest, and Helen found herself watching it explore the masculine undulations by now glistening with a light sheen of perspiration. She licked her lips, suddenly feeling parched. She jumped when Alex rolled lazily onto his side, dislodging the wandering bee, and meeting her wide green gaze with a sensuous challenge.

Helen and Alex aren't even touching each other, yet she's electrified by the sight of the bee wandering where, perhaps, she would like to wander. She *hears* the sultry hum of the bee, *sees* it alight on his chest, which glistens with perspiration, *feels* parched as a result and reacts to his sudden move.

Every scene should be explored for its sensory possibilities. In my book *Centrefold*, watching the hero eat a sandwich becomes a turn-on for the heroine:

Watching him excise a crescent of sandwich with his perfect white teeth, she felt an ache start up deep inside her. It was as if each bite was connecting with the tender skin of her neck. She could feel each nip, feel his firm mouth as it roved over her throat in a torrent of love bites. Suddenly his head came up and his eyes locked with hers, making her colour hotly as if she had somehow communicated her fantasy to him. But all he said was, 'I'm glad you came back today, Danielle.'

In *Man Without a Past*, the heroine, Gaelle Maxwell, is a genealogist. The hero, Dan Buckhorn, was a foundling and has no knowledge of his background. In this book, I did have them declare their love for each other, but only because I was able to supply a powerful reason to keep them apart. Gaelle has discovered that they are apparently brother and sister, making their love forbidden. By the time they learn of their common history, they are head over heels in love with each other, making their separation a source of torment rather than irritation for the reader. I kept the sexual tension high by having Dan make love to Gaelle with words when he can't with deeds:

She noticed that his knuckles were also white against the table edge and his whole body angled forward, as if he unconsciously strained to reach her.

His eyes locked with hers, their iridescence at once challenging and inviting. Suddenly he said, 'I'm kissing you now. Can you feel it?'

Her tongue darted across her top lip. 'Yes—oh, yes.'

'Now my arms are around you. Can you feel that?'

Miraculously, the warmth of them enfolded her and she nodded. 'I feel them.'

'Now your head is on my shoulder and your weight is braced against me. There, is that good?'

Her slight body shuddered as her imagination supplied the hardness of his physique aligned with hers. She half rose but Dan motioned her back. 'Stay there. Just feel what I tell you to feel.'

Obediently she had closed her eyes and travelled with him on a journey of the imagination, to heights of sensation she had never dreamed were possible. Perhaps in reality they would still be impossible, happening only in the realm of the mind.

Amazing things can happen 'in the realm of the mind', for that is the stage upon which your drama will be played out. American copywriter and radio producer Stan Freberg made his radio commercials vivid and dramatic to fully exploit the possibilities of radio. He believed that radio was a special medium which should stretch the imagination. Good romance writing should also stretch the imagination, making possible flights of fantasy which would be beyond the budgets and technical skills of television and film producers.

Love and sex

Romance novels were once described by an editor as 'hard-core decency'. This label hasn't fitted for more than two decades. If you have kept your reading up to date, you'll be aware of the changes in the genre over the years, starting with the evolution of the heroine from Cinderella figure to capable career woman with a mind of her own.

Along with these changes, and with changing social standards, has come the freedom to pursue a romance to its ultimate conclusion. Every imprint is different, and the publishers' tip sheets should guide you as to what is acceptable for a particular line. But these days it's perfectly acceptable for the hero and heroine to make love before the final commitment, and while a satisfactory resolution is a given, you don't automatically have to conclude with a proposal of marriage.

Writer Bobbie Cole says:

> The publishing industry has come to realise that women from Betty Crocker to Gidget to Murphy Brown to Moll Flanders have their place in our lives, and not all women are just one or the other of them. Any situation can be sexy if the characters involved bring that sex appeal to the table with them.

To show how sexual involvement would be different between published lines, Cole cites a typical scene where the hero and heroine prepare dinner together:

1   Couple fixing dinner because they have to eat—if there is emotion involved, could be any line including Inspirational romances.
2   Couple nibbling on one another as they cook, just sweet kisses and lots of emotion—Silhouette Romance, Harlequin Tender, etc.
3   They burn dinner while enraptured. Lots of groping—Silhouette Special Editions, Harlequin American.
4   She wonders if he'll kill her with the steak knife—Harlequin Intrigue or Silhouette Intimate Moments.
5   Forget about the food—Harlequin Temptation.
6   They make a meal of each other—Harlequin Blaze, Ellora's Cave.

So, depending on the line you're writing for, love scenes may go all the way from sweet glances to steamy sex as in Harlequin's Blaze line and books published by Ellora's Cave, which it describes as 'any work of literature that is both romantic and sexually explicit in nature'. Because of this divergence, romance publishers frequently apply descriptive marketing labels such as 'sweet' or 'spicy' so readers can make informed choices about the level of sexuality they are comfortable reading about.

Strictly inspirational

At the other end of the scale of sexual explicitness are the inspirational romances, defined by Romance Writers of America as romantic novels 'with religious faith as a significant element of the story'. This definition applies whether the books are 50 000-word category novels, such as Steeple Hill's Love Inspired line and Barbour Heartsong Presents, or longer more mainstream books. However, sensuality is invariably suggested rather than depicted. Writing guidelines for Steeple Hill's women's fiction program state, 'There should be no explicit sex in these stories, and a minimum of sensuality and sexual desire. And unless it is part of the struggle the protagonists face, there should be no premarital sex or graphic violence.' Some inspirational publishers prohibit any hint of sexual content whatsoever, including dancing scenes. Such requirements will be spelled out in their writers' guidelines, and evident from a study of their published books.

Sweet romances

'Sweet' usually describes the overall tone of a book, rather than a prescribed level of sexual involvement between the characters. Some lines, such as the majority of inspirationals and Silhouette romances, specify that the characters should not make love at all unless married. Other imprints may be more flexible, but, in all cases, for the book to qualify as a sweet romance, the couple will make love only when the heroine believes the hero is the one man for her, even if the relationship founders over some problem soon afterwards. At the time, she feels committed to him and the reader shares her feelings. If the characters make love, the emphasis will be on emotions and feelings rather than physical descriptions.

Every love scene in the book, whether it's a kiss or a fully fledged description of the characters making love, should be included because it advances the relationship, not because a certain number of pages have gone by without one. Each action the characters take should be justified in terms of where the relationship stands in the story. If she's screaming blue murder at him, he is unlikely to kiss her passionately unless given a good reason, such as to quieten her before someone overhears them. All of this should be made clear.

There should also be plenty of sparks and spice before—and during—lovemaking. This is your chance to build the sensual tension referred to previously. Let us share the heroine's feelings every step of the way. There is an obstacle between them, so giving in to her feelings involves a struggle with herself. It should not come about too quickly or too lightly. If she does capitulate, it's because what she feels is much more powerful than the reasons she shouldn't give in.

Afterwards she may have one of two reactions—either she's furious with herself for allowing her desires to overwhelm her commonsense or she's happy because she feels their relationship is on a new plane. Only later will she discover that it didn't change a thing, and that the barriers are still there between them. In sweet romances, if publishing guidelines permit the couple to make love, this, rather than sex, will be the important factor.

Where the line allows, I prefer my characters to dictate the nature of their own relationships, depending on how they feel about each other at a given time. I also prefer to delay having them make love, both to enable a sense of commitment to develop and to raise the reader's sense of anticipation.

All descriptions should emphasise what the characters—especially the heroine—are thinking and feeling. This is much more important than who is doing what to whom, or, as someone said, putting tab A into slot B. Incidentally, even in sweet romances, the heroine does not need to be a virgin. These days it takes an inventive writer to justify the existence of a virginal heroine in her 20s.

You do not need to mention harsh realities such as AIDS but you do need to be aware of their effect on reader attitudes. This awareness should be reflected in the way you handle your love scenes, by having your characters know one another more fully before making love or by having them share a common background so they already possess this knowledge. Otherwise, having them jump into bed together at the first opportunity can seem reckless.

Use of a condom usually needs to be mentioned or alluded to. It may be enough to suggest that the characters have 'taken precautions' or the hero has ensured that the heroine is 'protected'. In sweet romances the fantasy element needs to be preserved, and it can't be if too many harsh realities are allowed to intrude on what should be a beautiful, uplifting and emotionally involving moment for the reader.

Male writers sometimes have trouble writing sweet love scenes. They tend to concentrate on the physical details, when emotions and sensations should play the biggest part. This is also the area where new writers, both male and female, tend to rush things. In surveys that ask, 'What do women want from sex?' the answer is invariably, 'time and tenderness' in some guise, and this is what the reader seeks, too. Develop the scenes slowly, using sensuous, poetic words and phrases. Focus on the feelings and emotions of the characters, their thoughts, misgivings, hopes and dreams. The easiest way to avoid clichés is to write from inside your hero or heroine, letting us share their unique perspective.

Let them talk to each other. It's surprising how seldom the characters are allowed to speak to each other during love scenes, yet this is one way to show the growing under-standing between them. Build and build and build until the tension between them is almost unbearable. When they finally give in to their feelings, we're aroused right along with them. When they finally make love, it should be a beautiful, triumphant moment.

This rules out any suggestion of forced sex. The heroine must want the hero as much as he wants her, even if commonsense tells her she *shouldn't* want him. All she knows is that she does and her desire has a rightness about it which she cannot deny. If, afterwards, it turns out to be a mistake because of problems between them, she should not be aware of this at the time. The reader should feel that, in the same situation, she would do exactly the same thing.

This is how I build to a love scene in *Centrefold*:

Their hands were still linked, and he stroked her forearm slowly, sending shivers of sensation through her. She leaned towards him as if pulled on an invisible string, feeling fiercely hungry. But it was a hunger which no food could satisfy. Rowan's dark eyes slid over her, his expression telling her he felt the same way.

As one, they leaned closer, until their lips met across the table. Rowan's hands gripped her shoulders and she linked her arms around his neck. The edge of the table bit into her, and she pulled back reluctantly, grudging every inch which kept them apart.

Desire swept through her so strongly that, when she stood up, she had to hold on to the table for support. She nodded, not yet trusting her voice, which would surely betray her with its huskiness. She could feel her throat tight and her mouth dry, so that it was an effort to speak. 'I think we'd better have that swim, don't you?'

Her fingers were shaking so much that she had trouble changing into the bikini which Rowan had brought for her from the studio. It was crocheted from crimson cotton over a flesh-coloured lining, giving the impression that it was almost transparent. Catching sight of herself in it, in the changing-room mirror, she felt bold and wanton, understanding why the design was called 'Temptress'. It was exactly what she felt like.

This is only the beginning. After resisting his attraction successfully over lunch, she tries to have the swim they planned. Little by little, their desires overcome them and they end up making love at the shallow end of the pool.

In my early drafts of this chapter, the couple made love before they had the swim. The sexual tension was reduced because I hadn't given it sufficient chance to build to the maximum. Rewriting the chapter so that the lunch with all its promise comes first, followed by the swim, then at long last the love scene, has much more impact. Even then the final scene ran to another five printed pages. Anything less would have short-changed the reader.

From spicy to erotica

These are the hottest novels on the market today which can still be called romances. The Harlequin Blaze line has evolved out of the Temptation line and aims to showcase authors 'who have a strong sexual edge to their stories'.

The Blaze tip sheet uses descriptions such as 'sexy', 'sizzling', 'sensuous' and 'highly romantic', and seeks 'innovative plots that are sexy in premise and execution'. The tone of the books may run from fun and flirtatious to dark and sensual, and the hero and heroine should make a commitment at the end, although this does not necessarily mean a marriage proposal.

Ellora's Cave began as an e-publisher and now produces titles in electronic and paperback form, and is the first e-publisher to be recognised by Romance Writers of America. To achieve this recognition, a publisher must be a 'non-subsidy, non-vanity press that has released books on a regular basis via national (in the USA) distribution for a minimum of one year and has sold a minimum of 1,500 hardcover/trade paperback copies or 5,000 copies of any other format of a single fiction book or novella or collection of novellas in book form'. Ellora's Cave achieved this distinction by selling 1500 copies of *The Empress' New Clothes* by Jaid Black.

Its writers' guidelines say that 'sexual language is

typically expressed in frank adult terms, rather than couched in flowery phrases'. Novels are 'rated' according to the detail and length of love scenes and the language used to describe them. This grading enables readers to avoid material they may find objectionable, and guides writers in how far they can go.

The chick lit genre in which young women navigate the pitfalls of modern life falls somewhere between sweet and ultra-sexy romances. These books treat sexual encounters as part of ordinary life. Chick lit is rarely explicit, although they do describe sexual encounters in everyday language rather than poetic euphemism. Since they often concern the heroine's efforts to find Mr Right, or Mr Right for Now, they may also deal with sex in a more humorous, light-hearted fashion.

In order to be able to write convincing love scenes which engage the reader's emotions, you should develop your own sexual awareness. Reading about contemporary sexuality, and books like Beatrice Faust's *Women, Sex and Pornography* will widen the scope of your love scenes. This doesn't necessarily mean reaching for the kinky or unusual, unless this is a feature of the line you're writing for. But you need to be as creative with your love scenes as elsewhere in the story; perhaps more so, since so much has already been written.

Freshness and originality are always your goals. As a woman told me at a Perth seminar, she was tired of reading romance novels where the characters spent all their time in bed together. Braced for the worst, I asked her to explain. She said it would be more interesting if they sometimes made love on a riverbank in the moonlight, for a change.

Sexual tension checkpoints

Go through a piece of your own or your favourite author's writing. Look closely at how scenes between the hero and heroine are handled. How well are two or more of the senses used to transmit to the reader the heroine's reactions to the hero? Do you feel what she feels, or do you stay on the outside, having to be content with descriptions rather than being given the sensory clues you need to share her experiences?

Try writing or rewriting a meeting between your hero and heroine. Allow at least a page or longer to describe how they interact. What does she see and hear? Taste and smell? What does he say and how does he say it? What responses do his words and actions trigger deep inside the heroine?

Ideally, the response should be so powerful that it catches her by surprise. It happens in spite of any reasons she has not to be attracted to him, and she can't stop it from happening. Probably no other man has made her feel quite this way.

Incidentally, avoid phrases such as 'she had never been so overwhelmed in her life'. She can hardly have been overwhelmed in someone else's life or, as far as we know, before or after her own life. It is enough to say 'she had never felt so overwhelmed'. In the same vein, I'd rather not read 'she thought to herself'. Unless she is telepathic, she can't think to anyone else.

As editor Anne Gisonny says, 'The power of a story is in the telling of it, in the ability of the author to engage a reader's emotions and to convincingly portray a full spectrum of the human experience.'

3
Characterisation

*A*n author sent a manuscript to a publisher and, in the covering letter, stated that the characters were fictitious, bearing no resemblance to anyone either living or dead. The editor rejected the manuscript with the terse comment, 'That's what's wrong with it'.

Your characters should be so convincingly real that the reader comes to believe in their existence. People still write letters to Sherlock Holmes at his Baker Street, London, address, although neither the detective nor the address ever existed. Tourists visited outback Australia seeking Drogheda, the fictitious sheep station where *The Thorn Birds* (McCullough) is set. And the town of Tarzana, United States, was named after a character with a language deficiency and a penchant for swinging through trees. This is the power of fiction to conjure up characters who live in the imagination, if not in the real world. You may not recall any of Sherlock Holmes's adventures but you can probably picture the man himself, complete with deerstalker hat and meerschaum pipe, although in fact it was the illustrator who gave Holmes his famous hat. The plot details of *The Thorn Birds* may escape you but you will surely remember Meggie Cleary and Father Ralph. Scarlett and Rhett, Mr Rochester and Jane Eyre, Emma Harte from Margaret Taylor Bradford's *A Woman of Substance*, Lilian from *Lilian's Story* by Kate Grenville, all remain in the mind after the stories themselves are forgotten. Why?

As someone once said, fiction is folks. 'The dramatist's work area is people. Everything else is secondary,' said Gene Roddenberry, creator of the *Star Trek* universe. Have you ever watched a dramatic car chase on television with spectacular accidents, near misses, screeching of tyres, the whole package—and been bored witless? It happens because there is no-one you care about on the screen, so all the action leaves you unmoved. Watch a news item about a plane crash on another continent. You may be sad for the victims, yet your emotions are uninvolved. Yet watch the same news item when a member of your family is holidaying on that continent and you'll be riveted, fingers jammed against your mouth, heart racing. Someone you care about could be in jeopardy.

Every character needn't be in mortal danger for you to care what happens to them. They may be thwarted in getting their heart's desire or kept apart from someone they love. You'll be there on the sidelines, cheering for them and sharing every moment of their struggle against the odds.

Just as you can't truly mourn for strangers in a plane crash other than as fellow human beings, you can't share the struggles of fictitious characters unless you have come to know them. As in real life, it takes a while to get to know someone. First you see their physical characteristics and draw some conclusions about the type of person they are. Then you get to know them, little by little, until they are as fully revealed to you as another person can be. In fiction there's the added advantage of being able to share the character's innermost thoughts and feelings. In real life you can only guess how they feel or be guided by what the person chooses to tell you.

People read fiction in order to live for a while inside another person's skin, in a way which is impossible in real life.

To make people care about what happens to your characters you have to create *real people*, or at least the semblance of them. Characters should not be lifted wholly from among your friends and acquaintances. Apart from the horrendous legal implications if your friends don't like what you write, fictitious characters need to be larger than life. Even if they are dull, they must be super-dull. They must be truly unforgettable.

Romance writing offers a unique challenge. Because of the built-in restrictions of the genre it is a real art to create unique heroes and heroines who will live on in readers' minds. So much has already been said and done in romance fiction that you have to work hard at creating new and different heroes and heroines who still 'fit' the requirements of romance.

A judge at the Romance Writers' Golden Heart Awards (then known as the Golden Medallion), Roy Sorrels, says that too many characters *read* like romance heroes and heroines, as if the writer had sent over to 'Central Casting' with a request for a set of stock characters and stock situations. In these stories, the characters meet on cue and are instantly attracted. The reader never understands why they are attracted to each other. They dislike one another on sight and yet proceed to fall in love. This isn't a romance novel. This is a pastiche, but, too often, it's what new writers think romance publishers want to see. They are wrong.

Today's romance publishers are more flexible than ever. The days of the naive teenage heroine and the worldly wise 30-year-old tycoon are long gone. Characters are closer together in age and experience; women have demanding, even masculine-sounding careers. It's the difference between a woman *needing* a man to make her life worth living and *wanting* a life partner with whom to share the ups and downs. She can live without him but she wouldn't want to. She should have a life before he comes along and not just be waiting around for Mr Right. He is certainly special but she should not have been living in limbo. Depending on the requirements of the line you're writing for, she may have had relationships or a marriage before the story begins. In chick lit and single-title romances, the characters may be involved in more than one relationship, and the reader may have to guess which man will turn out to be Mr Right or Mr Right for Now.

In my first published romance, *Love's Greatest Gamble*, Sabrina is a widow in her early 30s, bringing up her child alone. Her late husband, a victim of war neurosis, was a compulsive gambler and has left her with huge debts of which she is unaware until Keenan Royce, a casino boss, comes to collect the money. To protect her daughter's memories of her father, Sabrina agrees to do whatever Keenan demands to repay the debt.

In *That Midas Man*, the heroine is involved in a custody battle with her former husband who has turned out to be a scoundrel of the first order. Her wish to regain custody of her child motivates her actions in the story. Market research shows that babies are one of the most popular elements in romance novels, perhaps because many readers are parents or single parents themselves and can empathise with the heroine's struggles, or may have chosen not to have children, preferring to read about them instead.

The quality of empathy is vitally important. It is not to be confused with sympathy, which means having compassion for someone with a problem. Empathy involves literally projecting yourself inside the other person and feeling as they do, which is the ideal you're trying to achieve.

The wonderful result of creating well-rounded characters is the way they drive the story forward with very little persuasion from the author. Because the heroine is a certain kind of person, such-and-such happens to her. She reacts in accordance with the personality you've developed for her, which leads naturally to another situation and another reaction, and so on. This is what writers describe as the characters 'taking over the story', and you can make it happen once you know the secret. All you have to do is give the character a certain nature, then let her act in accordance with that nature. Someone you've established as timid and shy would never bounce up on stage in front of hundreds of people to announce that a guest speaker hasn't turned up. She may have to be prodded on stage and may be struck dumb until the hero jumps up beside her. His presence reassures her, making it easy and natural for her to say what she must.

This is what editors call 'inevitability'—the opposite of contrivance. Because of the kind of people you've created, things can't happen any other way. Of course, all novels are contrived, but your job is to make them look as if they aren't.

You'll begin to gather that the author can only invent characters up to a point. Once you decide on certain characteristics, others must follow for the story to have the ring of truth. I used to think that science fiction writers had it easy, being able to create whole worlds where almost anything could happen. However, studying the medium reveals that science fiction writers are no freer to invent worlds than we romance writers are. The moment one aspect of a world is decided, others automatically follow. Speculate that a planet is larger than Earth, say, and straightaway it must have stronger gravity—at least according to known science. This rules out tall, thin inhabitants, since stronger gravity would pull them downwards, creating heavier, squatter beings. As science fiction writer Jerry Pournelle points out in *The Craft of Science Fiction*, 'A writer may choose any social order he pleases . . . Having chosen it, though, he has lost part of his freedom.'

It's also important not to make your characters too perfect. Readers won't identify with someone who never puts a foot wrong, who gets out of bed before the alarm rings every morning, jogs 5 kilometres, then eats a healthy breakfast, shrugs into any old garment at hand but looks like a fashion model, skips make-up because her sparkling eyes and perfect skin don't need such artifice, then heads off to her job as defence counsel for the poor and oppressed. Naturally, she doesn't need the work, since she's heir to Daddy's hair-dye fortune. No-one is going to believe in such a paragon, far less empathise with her.

Better to have her sleep through the alarm, spring out of bed in horror because she's in danger of losing her job, which she needs to pay for singing tuition if she's ever to escape this grind. Rushing breakfast, she sets fire to the bacon, which brings the hero dashing in to douse the flames. Which heroine are you more likely to relate to? And which provides the more interesting story possibilities?

Remember, your characters do not have to be perfect—just perfect for each other. So how do you go about creating them? A Chinese proverb holds that the beginning of wisdom is to call things by their right names, which is as good a place as any to start people-building.

Naming the baby

Some writers still adhere to the romance tradition of giving characters outlandish names. I tend to go with what sounds right for a particular character. There's nothing wrong with naming your characters Tom, Dick, Harry and Jane. It's preferable to having character names that are so bizarre they grate on the reader from beginning to end. When this happens, the author risks losing the reader's empathy, so the names aren't serving the book. A middle course, where the names are special enough to be memorable, yet not so bizarre that they annoy the reader, is probably best.

Sound and rhythm are good guides when choosing names. Try saying the full name aloud, letting your ears guide you. Surnames of one syllable, such as Brown, Jones, Lane and so on, usually sound best with a given name of two or more syllables. Coralie Lane, for example, sounds more lyrical than Cora Lane.

Surnames of two syllables combine well with first names of three syllables. In *Man and Wife*, the hero's surname is Monroe and his first name is Christopher. With a three-syllable surname like Dominick (the heroine of the same book), a first name of one syllable sounded best, so I called her Drew, a feminine form of her father's name, Andrew. If the surname is short, make the first name longer, as in Gemma Tate from *Snowy River Man* and Tanith Page in *The Leopard Tree*. (I chose Tanith because it is another name for Astarte, ancient goddess of the moon; my Tanith is a UFO enthusiast.) Names usually sound best when the number of syllables in the first name and surname are unequal. Avoid confusion by having dissimilar names—Paul and John, rather than Jack and John or John and Joan.

The name should be spelled much as it is pronounced, to avoid embarrassing readers. This is especially important if the name appears in the title. Imagine having to go into a bookshop and ask for a book with a title you can't pronounce.

In many of the traditional romance lines, your hero and heroine will agree to marry at the end of the book. What will her first name sound like when joined with his surname (assuming she will change her name)? This used to be a popular pastime on television comedy shows. If Rose Smith married Peter Bush, she'd be Rose Bush . . . and so on. Most single women try out their married names well before the proposal, and so should your heroine.

If there's an interesting reason behind the character's name, so much the better. Drew Dominick is the 'son' her father longed for, brought up to succeed him as head of a huge corporation. Her lack of traditional feminine upbringing and inclinations is a cornerstone of the story, so everything ties together neatly.

Tanith Page's name also gives rise to some provocative dialogue:

Besides, giving him her name wasn't going to make her predicament any worse than it already was. 'Tanith Page,' she admitted.

'Ah, Tanith, worshipped by the Carthaginians as Astarte, goddess of the moon,' he said appreciatively.

> She hoped he didn't also know that Astarte was the goddess of fertility. At high school, Tanith had been teased unmercifully when her classmates discovered that part.

Names can come from all sorts of sources. Some writers swear by baby-naming books. My personal favourite is the credits at the end of American television programs. With its enormous cultural diversity, the United States seems to have a greater variety of names than any other country. Try it and see! Other sources include the Internet, telephone books and maps. When I needed a royal family name for my Sapphan books, set in a fictitious kingdom in the Andaman Sea, I took names from streets found in maps of the region. My Carramer books, published by Silhouette, are set against a French–Polynesian background, so I downloaded lists of French names from the Internet, while the name of Carramer's royal family, de Marigny, was one I spotted on television for only a few seconds.

When you come across an interesting name, write it down and file it away. Sometimes, the name itself will suggest a story direction.

A woman with a male-sounding name still has lots of story possibilities, even if some variations have been done to death. These days it's no longer acceptable to have a man object to a woman's presence merely because he was expecting a man to turn up. There should be a stronger reason why the mix-up is a problem. In *A Fair Exchange*, my American heroine's nickname is Jake, short for Jacqueline. She is visiting Australia on an agricultural exchange program but her host family has a medical emergency while she's en route to Australia. Exchange trainees are billeted with married couples for obvious reasons, so the heroine's gender is a real problem when her surrogate host turns out to be a very eligible bachelor. Even then, she is able to stay with him under certain conditions, but I got some interesting mileage out of the mix-up with her name in the early part of the book.

Know your characters inside and out

A brilliant and perceptive editor at Mills & Boon, the late Jacqui Bianchi, told me that far too many books sound as if the characters were born on page one. They have no family, no history, nothing to make a reader feel as if they could live outside the pages of the book. To create what editors call a 'well-rounded character', you need to provide both an inner and outer view. The outer view includes the physical description of the character—age, hair colour and style, eye colour, build. There are lots of ways to get this information across, most commonly by having the character look into a mirror or see their reflection in a shop window. The details can also be conveyed through the eyes of another character, enabling you to suggest aspects of the person's nature beyond the physical, as in this example from *The Baron and the Bodyguard*:

> This time he was able to force his eyes open, and saw a vision bending over him. Jacinta. A head sculpted by Michelangelo was capped with shining blonde hair, neat except for a few stray wisps curling across her forehead and around her ears. The effect suggested an abandoned nature kept under firm control, but not quite. His blurred gaze gave him an imperfect view of her unusual gray-blue eyes, enough to see that they glistened, as if she was trying not to cry.

Another way to get the details across in a natural way without having the heroine seem vain is to have her see her own features as shortcomings, as I did in this passage from *Return to Faraway*:

> Examining herself critically in her mirror, she was thankful for the flaws in the glass which prevented her from studying herself too closely.
>
> Her hair was undoubtedly her best feature. It was a lustrous dark brown which she occasionally highlighted with a touch of henna. She made the most of her natural curls by wearing her hair in a mass of loose, pretty waves swept high off her face and kept in place by tortoiseshell combs or, more often, by a pair of sunglasses perched on her head.
>
> Apart from that, her own judgment was that she was too short, although luckily she was trimly built to compensate, with legs which Rona said had no right to be so long and slender on someone so diminutive. Shan had long ago decided that her nose was too crooked and her eyes were too close together—a verdict hotly denied by everyone else who knew her, especially her male admirers. There were still a few, despite the fact that she had a failed marriage behind her, she thought ruefully.

Another technique involves stepping out of the heroine's viewpoint for a few lines, long enough to describe her from the outside, as in this passage from *Heartbreak Plains*:

> If she had cared to look at her reflection in the plate-glass window at her back, she would have seen what passers-by found so appealing, a coltish, long-legged blonde with golden shoulder-length hair cut in a straight fringe over a wide forehead which sloped down to where honey-gold

lashes rested like silk fringes on tanned cheeks. When she did turn large, innocent blue eyes towards the window, it was not to study her own reflection. Instead, she peered through the window, trying to locate Barbara among the racks of clothes.

Note that I slide back into my heroine's point of view as soon as I can after getting the physical details implanted. But how do you arrive at a physical description of a character in the first place? A favourite method is to flip through magazines until you find a picture which fits your mental idea of the character. If the story is about a businesswoman, she will look different from a jillaroo.

When you've been writing for a while, you soon exhaust your mental stock of colourings and hairstyles. Hair-care magazines abound at newsagents. Stock up on several and note how the hairstyles are described as well as how they are created. For example, a hairstyle magazine might offer this description:

> Sleek, glossy hair falls straight down from a left-hand-side parting. The ends have been cut perfectly straight. Long hair like this must be looked after properly: wash it often, dry it gently and treat it to regular conditioning.

This could translate into the following scene:

> Jenny swung her long, glossy hair back from her shoulders, tucking the strands behind her left ear in an automatic gesture. Not for the first time, she wondered whether she would have it cut short. Matthew would hate it, but he wasn't the one who had to spend hours washing, drying and conditioning the wretched stuff.

By salting the physical details in among her own views, the reader is given a clue to Jenny's personality. She wears her hair long to please someone else. What does this say about her as a person? Another kind of person might enjoy the feel of the wind rippling her long hair until it streams out behind her like a silken parachute:

> Matthew had been nagging her for ages to have her hair cut short, complaining about the time it took to wash, dry and condition. But she had changed herself in so many ways to please him that if she gave in on this point, there wouldn't be much left of Jenny Holden.

Try a few experiments like this yourself. Describe your heroine's physical characteristics as accurately and vividly as you can. Is her hair brown, ash blonde, silver ash, medium brown or light brunette? Are her eyes blue, teal, steely grey or aqua? Are the colours clear or do they contain flecks of green or gold?

How tall is your character? Bear in mind that short and tall are relative terms. Tall is usually anyone taller than you are, ditto for short. Therefore, it is useful to describe characters' heights in relation to each other or to some physical feature, such as a doorway. This lets the reader 'see' the information rather than being presented with it by the author. In *A Fair Exchange*, the heroine, Jake, feels that her height puts her at a disadvantage in a confrontation with the hero:

> Jake's chin tilted defiantly as she strained to minimise the difference in height between them. But a tilted chin did little to make up for a six-inch variation in their heights.

In the same book, when they're walking side by side, height influences their respective strides:

> Taking two steps to every long-legged stride of his, she wondered what it would be like to go out on a real date with him. Would he keep a swathe of path between them as he was doing now, or would he match his stride to hers, dropping an arm around her shoulders to draw her closer?

Having pictured your character's appearance as vividly as you can, go on to decide on the character's likes and dislikes, again being as specific and detailed as possible. Complete a chart for each of your two major characters. Don't worry if you can't yet fill in every space. As you come to know the characters better, more of these details will come to mind. But try to be as thorough as you can. You probably won't use half of this information in the book but you, as the author, must know your characters intimately, in order to know how they would behave in different situations. Some of the best story possibilities arise out of the characters themselves, as you'll discover when you explore the characters' inner selves.

External profile

(Create one for each main character)

> Name
> Reasons for name (if any)
> Age and occupation
> Height and build
> Hair colour

Eye colour
Skin tones, distinguishing features

Family details:
Mother's name and occupation
Father's name and occupation
Still living or how died
Brothers? Names
Sisters? Names
Place in family
Childhood happy or unhappy? Why?

Education/professional training
Star sign
Previous relationships, if any
Where living and why
What kind of car and why
Favourite things (foods, hobbies, books)
Favourite personal possession

Getting inside your characters

All human beings have their share of fears. They also have hopes and dreams, values and quite a few regrets. Yet in romance writing, especially in first novels, too many characters are born, as Jacqui Bianchi said, on page one with none of the qualities which make a character come alive in the reader's mind.

Have you ever watched a film or read a story where the hero risked life and limb to achieve something, yet you had no clear idea why? In real life, someone might rush into a burning building and rescue a total stranger, but in fiction they need a strong reason to make the action seem believable—in other words, a motive. The *Pocket Oxford*

Dictionary defines a motive as 'productive of motion or action, what impels a person to action, fear, ambition or love'. Any of these motives could impel the person to enter the burning building, depending on the nature of the individual. A soldier might have regaled his girlfriend with stories about his war exploits, then be forced to enter the burning building rather than reveal that none of the exploits ever happened; he is really a coward. His motive is fear of revealing his true nature, possibly losing his girl. He could be a minor athlete who hopes that acclaim as a hero will improve his status. This is ambition at work. A nun or priest who passes the burning building might respond to cries for help out of selfless love, as professed in their religious vows.

You can see how important it is to know the characters before you begin to write their story. Only when you know what drives them can you possibly imagine what they might do and why. Once you know why, you can share their inner thoughts and feelings with the reader as they rush into the building, seek out and rescue the victim. The fearful soldier will think more about getting out alive, perhaps wishing he'd been more honest with his girlfriend. He is unlikely to be gentle with the victim, whom he probably blames for his predicament. The ambitious athlete will be watching for the TV cameras, wondering how he will look, and making sure that the victim, and anyone else nearby, knows his name. The religious person would have little thought of self and would probably pray for strength, and for the victim, while searching through the smoke and rubble.

In real life, actions don't always make sense. In fiction, they must. Every action and emotion you attribute to your character must have a motive behind it, in keeping with the kind of person you have created. Even your villains must have a good reason for their villainy. I once discussed the criminal mind with a policeman of some 30 years' experience. According to him, criminals frequently blame their victims for what befalls them. If someone is foolish enough to keep money in the house, they must expect to be robbed, according to criminals' logic. To them, victims deserve all they get. The criminals see themselves as merely taking advantage of an opportunity.

In *Return to Faraway*, my heroine's marriage had once been wrecked by the behaviour of the hero's teenage daughter from his first marriage. An attempt to patch things up is again jeopardised by the daughter and we learn that she blames the heroine for the failure of her parents' marriage, making her actions justified in her own eyes.

The classic 'other woman' in *Boss of Yarrakina* turns out to be afraid for her future. Her brother is likely to inherit the family property so she needs to make a marriage which will secure her prospects. She sees the heroine as a threat to her plans for herself and the hero. By giving every character in your book equally good reasons for their actions (motivation), you make your book come to life. Characters who are all good, all bad or stereotyped make a book shallow and unconvincing.

How do you create well-rounded characters? First, you must develop a genuine interest in other people. You can't write about real people unless you know them and understand why they do what they do. I recommend having many interests outside the writing sphere. Go to public meetings, even those concerning causes with which you don't identify. If you're a conservationist, attend pro-logging meetings and listen without arguing the issues in your own mind. Be open to both sides of a question. Go to college open days and find out what concerns people of generations other than your own. Talk to people much older and much younger than yourself. Don't reveal your purpose and don't take notes until you're back at your desk, to avoid making your contacts self-conscious. Your aim is to find out what they really think and why, so you have access to many more points of view than your own.

Every month I buy magazines outside my normal interest range, everything from *Playboy* to *Agricultural Digest* and pop-rock magazines. Apart from widening your view of the world, these can spark ideas outside your own range of experiences. An article about a farm secretary who divided her time among several outback properties inspired the idea for the heroine in *Man Shy*. I wrote to the woman interviewed in the article asking for further information. But for that issue of *Farm Journal*, I would not have known such a profession existed. Reading someone's sweatshirt at an exercise class gave me the idea for *A Fair Exchange*. Until then I had no idea that thousands of Australian farmers go to work on foreign farms every year while their foreign counterparts come to Australia to work and learn. A writer must be a sponge, soaking up ideas at every opportunity.

Popular psychology books are among the most useful reference books you can have on your bookshelf. Books like Thomas Harris's *I'm OK, You're OK* and Robin Norwood's *Women Who Love Too Much* give fascinating insights into how the past can influence behaviour in the present. These books are easier to understand and more fun to read than psychology texts, and the case histories are bound to provide more story ideas than you can use. Just to dip into one book at random: *In and Out of Love* by David Lewis explores 'the mystery of personal attraction'. Opening it at random, I came upon this paragraph:

> Suppose for instance you meet 8 new people per month and find half of them attractive. You approach a quarter of these and get your request for a date accepted 50% of the time. Your track record shows that one out of ten dates leads to a more lasting relationship.

This paragraph is surrounded by mathematical data related to the probability of tracking down the perfect partner. Now suppose that my heroine is disillusioned about love, perhaps because of a past disappointment. She makes it her business to prove that true love is statistically a myth. As a psychologist, she uses her training to prove her thesis. All goes well until she meets the hero in the course of her research. What then? *Voilà!* A plot is born out of randomly turning the pages of a popular psychology book.

Astrology texts can also provide clues to character, but since there are only twelve star signs, this has its limitations. Here's what Kisha's *Fun With the Stars* has to say about Gemini:

> The Gemini has a quick, restless look, with keen, sharp-looking eyes and a rather open face, with a smile which is always ready to burst through. The walk is quick and almost rushing, very often clumsy because there is so much on your mind that your body cannot keep up with your brain.

And on attitude to life:

Your attitude to life is one of curiosity, you must know what is happening around you, and your need for excitement will always lead you into trouble.

We also find that, according to this book anyway, the Gemini person is attracted by imagination and intellect rather than physical traits. Aquarians give such people greatest scope for expressing their inner nature. Cue the Aquarian hero.

Every character should have a distinctive personality and be an individual. I concede that this is difficult when so much is taken for granted about a romance hero or heroine, but it is worth striving for the ideal.

One way to evoke a strong emotional response in your reader is to give your character a passion for something: life, an ideal, a lover. In chick lit, her passion may be for the perfect pair of shoes or the ideal apartment. But beware of swapping stereotypes—Cinderella for the woman driven by her career, for example.

Tanith Page's passion for UFOs, which brings her out to a lonely property at night, makes her individual. She may be beautiful, feisty and career-oriented in the best romantic tradition, but her one oddity is what makes her special and brings her into headlong conflict with the hero. At the same time, her passion for stargazing is firmly based in her past. When she was a teenager, her father was crippled when his jeweller's shop was robbed. After that, the family had no time for anything but his needs, so Tanith turned to the stars for consolation.

In *The Baron and the Bodyguard*, Jacinta is determined never to be helpless again, after seeing a man she loved killed and being unable to help him when she was a teenager. Her determination is reflected not only in her choice of career as a martial arts teacher and bodyguard, but in her reluctance to relinquish control of her emotions to the hero.

All the character details out of which these plots arose would have been included in character profile charts like those in this chapter. It is important to complete them as fully and thoughtfully as you can for each of your major characters. Don't be afraid to use reference works like astrology or pop psychology books to expand on your own knowledge. As long as you draw only *ideas* from these books and don't borrow another author's words and phrases, the use is legitimate. My idea of a statistician researching romance was triggered by David Lewis's book, but my handling of it would be my own.

Once you've worked out an internal and external profile for each character, you might like to try a method used by many writers, including Gene Roddenberry, creator of *Star Trek*. To persuade his characters to 'become real', as he put it, he drew a line down the centre of a sheet of paper, writing his questions on the left and the characters' 'answers' on the right. He said the list of questions sometimes ran to hundreds of pages and the answers often surprised him; indeed at times the characters would end up asking *him* questions.

When he conceived Mr Spock, the logical Vulcan, he asked the character, 'What is the universe for? What is its function?' Mr Spock's answer, written in the right-hand column, said that the universe is a giant life- and intelligence-producing machine. This answer was so Spock-like that Roddenberry added it to his production notes. Later, he discovered that this view of the universe is a cornerstone of some Eastern philosophies; he had probably read it somewhere and it had re-emerged out of his subconscious.

There's nothing spiritual or metaphysical about this kind of dialogue, Roddenberry said. It is merely a process of using the imagination to tap into new areas of memory, new logic circuits in the brain. If it can result in a character as memorable as Mr Spock, it's worth a try. When using this technique, write your questions and answers as quickly as you can and try not to guide or censor your responses. If kept up for long enough, this method can be surprisingly revealing.

So your characters need a past and a future, likes and dislikes, and strong opinions about their world. What else will bring them to life in your book? The answer is goals. Author Gary Provost pins a note above his desk which asks, 'What does this character want?' Once you can answer this question you are close to establishing the plot of your romance novel.

It's tempting to say that a romance heroine wants to find happiness. Very well, what would make her happy? Not long ago I attended a seminar at which we were asked to set our own goals for the short, medium and long term. Many participants said they wanted plenty of money or financial security. They were then asked how much money they would need to make them feel secure, turning the goal into a specific rather than a general one. A specific goal is also more attainable: 'a million dollars' is easier to measure than 'enough money'.

Try to specify precisely what would make your heroine happier than she is at the start of the book. Beware of setting her goal as 'to find true love'. Love should not be her main goal, otherwise she is likely to spend the entire book agonising over whether the hero will love her or not. She should start the book with a goal in the form of a problem she needs to solve *in order* to be happy. This gives direction and pace to the story as we wait to see whether she will get what she wants/find the treasure/save the ancestral home.

Ideally, the hero will be the one standing in her way. Although she's attracted to him from the first, she can't give in to her feelings without sacrificing her goal. Solving the problem is then essential if she is to become free to love. This prevents the characters mooning around with no sense of direction for pages on end. If the hero is part of the problem or, better still, if the hero *is* the problem, the quest becomes a real page-turner. Will she sacrifice her goal for love? Will she reach her goal but lose her chance at happiness with the hero? This may sound self-evident, but it also gives you something to write about.

In each of my books, the heroine starts off with a problem, which she is about to solve when an obstacle arises in the form of the hero and his wants. Putting the goals of hero and heroine on a collision course, complicated by their attraction for each other, is what makes a book sing.

Operation Monarch

Problem   The black sheep hero may be the true heir to the Carramer throne, the villain keeping his existence secret until revealing it can do the most harm to the kingdom.

Solution   The heroine, a royal investigator, must guard him while establishing the truth of his heritage.

Obstacle   As a teenager she was in love with him until he broke her heart. Now their renewed passion threatens her carefully planned life.

Tasmanian Devil

Problem The heroine is a prisoner of her father's fortune.

Solution She agrees to spend a month fending for herself on an island to earn the right to an independent life.

Obstacle The hero's presence on the island puts her goal at risk.

A Fair Exchange

Problem The shock discovery in adulthood that she is adopted makes the heroine ask who she really is.

Solution She travels to Australia to find her roots.

Obstacle The hero doesn't want her to expose the long-held secret of his sister's adoption.

Man and Wife

Problem The heroine feels that as a single professional woman, she gets a worse domestic deal than a man would.

Solution She decides to hire a man as her 'wife'.

Obstacle The 'wife' turns out to be her industrial rival, who has his own reasons for taking the job.

Man Without a Past

Problem After an out-of-character fling, the heroine finds herself pregnant.

Solution So her baby can know its father, she must track down her lover, who has disappeared.

Obstacle He doesn't want her around because his life is in danger.

You should be able to break down the plot of your novel into these three steps. Designing an internal and external profile of each character is the first step. When you have decided what the heroine wants (her goal or problem), you can map out a solution for her. The above examples should give you an idea of how this works. In every romance book it is a given that the hero and heroine will be strongly attracted to each other. The problem and her solution, which is at odds with what he wants, is what will keep them apart for 50 000 or more words. It's also great fun.

Not just any goal will do. In *Making a Good Script Great*, Linda Seger says a goal must do three things:

♥ convince the audience that a great deal will be lost if the character does not attain the goal

♥ bring the protagonist [your heroine] into direct conflict with the goals of the antagonist [the hero]

♥ be sufficiently difficult to achieve that the character [the heroine] changes while moving towards the goal.

This character change is an important cornerstone of successful fiction. If your characters are the same at the end of the story as they are at the beginning, little has been achieved. Your characters must learn and grow from their experiences. In the end, they will be better, stronger people for overcoming their obstacles. Their reward is a lifetime of happiness together.

To be believable, this change must happen gradually. In *Operation Monarch*, the hero is a black sheep with a basic distrust of people. Through the actions of the heroine in clearing his name, he learns to trust again. In *The Prince and the Marriage Pact*, the heroine believes that royalty is trouble after her mother became pregnant to a prince's equerry who then abandoned her. In discovering her true heritage, the heroine learns not to judge individuals by their titles.

In Charles Dickens's immortal *A Christmas Carol*, Scrooge changes gradually from a miser to a philanthropist with each new experience shown to him by the ghosts. If there was no evidence that their messages were reaching him, the change would not be believable. With a hero who has to learn to trust, his transformation can be shown little by little, through his actions and his conversations with the heroine. The change must happen gradually, logically, from scene to scene.

In *Tasmanian Devil*, the heroine, Evelyn, wants to be more than a decoration. To earn the right to a place in her father's corporation, she volunteers to spend a month fending for herself on an island willed to her by her mother. Unbeknown to her, Dane Balkan has leased the other cottage on the island and refuses to leave. When Evelyn offers to buy out his lease, she confirms his opinion that she is no better than his ex-wife, who was also rich and made his life miserable. He is determined to avoid her kind again. The attraction between them is strong, of course—this is a romance—but they both resist it because giving in would mean betraying their goals. Gradually, they learn that their love is possible, but not without ups and downs. In one important transformation scene, they have finally given in to their mutual sexual attraction and made love. Their goals are still in conflict, however:

> 'I don't want you to make love to me,' she insisted, trying to make the lie sound convincing. She did want him to make love to her, but she wanted much more which he wasn't prepared to give.
>
> 'You wanted me to last night.'
>
> Last night was different. Couldn't he see that?

Evidently he couldn't. 'You were able to forget that I was out of your class,' he reminded her.

She shook her head impatiently. 'Yes, but I can't forget that I'm out of yours.'

His eyes darkened with confusion. 'You aren't making sense. How could you be out of my class?'

'Easily. You're everything I dream of being—strong, independent. You know what you want from your life and how to get it.' Her voice tailed away on a sigh of despair.

'Surely you could be all those things if you wanted to?'

She chewed her lower lip thoughtfully. 'It isn't so easy after a lifetime of being conditioned to conform.'

His look of puzzlement turned to anger as he released her and walked away. 'Well, it's nice to know I've been part of your emancipation.'

His derisive tone sliced through her like a knife. 'You're determined to see me in the worst possible light, aren't you?' she demanded. Tears clustered at the backs of her eyes and she blinked furiously. He wasn't going to make her cry, damn him. 'Can't you see, you're equally guilty of snobbery?'

He swung around, his lip curling into a sneer. 'Well at least it's more honest than your kind of snobbery.'

With hands on hips and legs wide apart, she faced him like a cornered animal, a wild creature fighting for survival. 'Is it? I'm here, aren't I? I slept on a rug on the floor of your cabin, wrapped in a blanket. What's snobbish about that?'

He stared at her in astonishment, the anger in his eyes turning amazingly to respect. Then she was stunned to hear him laugh, the sound rich and rolling, reaching out to her in a caress of sound. 'Your behaviour was as unspoilt as could be, except for one thing.'

'What's that?' she asked, intrigued.

'You were right about sleeping on the floor in a blanket but you did it wearing a Cartier watch.'

This scene provides glimpses of the changes which will eventually take place in both characters. Brought up to conform, Evelyn has already broken with tradition by sleeping with Dane at all, let alone on a rug on a cabin floor. The watch symbolises the part of her that has yet to change. She is so used to wearing it that she doesn't notice it, but he does. He sees it as a status symbol and a symbol of everything which stands between them. However, he is also changing, little by little. This scene comes about halfway through the book. Her defiance earns his grudging respect. When these two finally resolve their differences, the reader should have no difficulty in understanding what they see in each other.

Too many books *tell* us the characters are attracted to each other when they should *show* us what they find fascinating about each other, so we can understand how they come to fall in love.

At the beginning of *Operation Monarch*, Gage dislikes what Serena stands for, equating her with the model he knew as a teenager. As he gets to know her all over again, he learns that she has qualities worthy of his love. Serena is strong, courageous and goal-driven, just like Gage himself. I don't need to tell the reader this. It is shown in how they interact, for example when she is prepared to dive with Gage because he needs her, although she admits she is terrified of sharks.

How do you bring about a change in your character as the story progresses? Start by looking at the problem the heroine has to solve. In Serena's case, she has to let go of her preconceptions about Gage, while showing him that she is no longer the self-centred teenage model he once knew. To do this she has to work alongside him while accepting him as he is. The character change is part and parcel of her achieving her goal.

In *Operation Monarch*, Serena discovers that Gage may be assisting the group seeking to undermine the monarchy, a fact he has kept from her. She sees this as an attempt to sabotage her work. In a lesser person, such a discovery would have ended any hope of a future relationship. In Serena, it only makes her more determined to establish the truth, assisting in her transformation.

In *Man and Wife*, corporate head, Drew Dominick wants to achieve a better balance between her career and her home life. She starts with her life out of balance— demonstrated when her housekeeper walks out and Drew ruins a dress when she tries to iron it herself. To reach her goal, she has to change from a career-centred person to a more well-rounded individual.

In each case, once you know what problem your heroine wants to solve, you can decide what is lacking in her personality and what changes she will have to undergo to achieve her goal. The story should provide opportunities for her to change and also obstacles which make it harder and harder for her to reach her goal, until it looks as if she will never change enough to get what she wants.

Bring on the hero

It's no accident that most of what's been said refers to the heroine's goals and motivations. Romance readers are almost exclusively female and, in the main, want to live their heroine's adventures, vicariously falling in love with the hero. So the heroine's goals and motivations are primary. However, this doesn't mean you can get away with a cardboard cut-out hero who acts and talks tough before tossing the heroine onto his bed. Years ago he may have been such a man, but times have changed and, with them, the romance hero. These days heroes must have emotions, weaknesses and dreams, just as heroines can be portrayed as strong, reasoning and capable.

There is a difference between having weaknesses and being weak. Alan Boon, son of the founder of Mills & Boon, told me his company had 'tried out more wimpish heroes'. It has also tried 'blond, Scandinavian types', but he said they have never taken off. Could this be because, in attempting to escape the tall, dark and handsome stereotype, some writers went too far in the opposite direction? What came out were sensitive 'New Age' men who had nothing remotely heroic about them.

I prefer a middle course, with heroes who are strong and self-reliant without being boorish in their treatment of other people. If the hero is well motivated, with a goal of his own to work towards, he will be both heroic and believable. Like the heroine, he needs a past which influences his behaviour in the present. In older romances, he would probably have been dark and brooding, with very little explanation of how he got that way.

The hero too must have a problem to solve, a goal he is striving for. When it comes to his relationship with the heroine, the hero must treat her with respect even if they dislike each other. Forced sex or any kind of abuse is out. The 'bodice-ripper' type of romance was mercifully short-lived and is not acceptable to modern readers. If the hero and heroine make love, it should be because they both want to, even if she knows she shouldn't want to. While your characters can change in any number of ways to become better than they are at the start of your story, it is not acceptable to have them change from abusive or violent to Mr Nice Guy.

I try to give my heroes a touch of intrigue, a sense of past tragedy if at all possible. This makes their change one of 'darkness into light'. In *Operation Monarch*, the hero is adopted, and there is serious doubt about his true parentage. This lack of a past becomes his past, motivating him in the present. He refuses to risk loving anyone until the uncertainty surrounding his identity is resolved.

Does a hero have to be tall, dark and handsome? Well, yes and no. These days, heroes come in all shapes and sizes, but the vast majority are still you-know-what. Just as women's magazines know their sales will increase if they put photographs of certain people on the cover, so the dark hero usually wins over the blond one in romance-novel cover illustrations. Nevertheless, you can strive for originality when it comes to describing your hero. I like the description of the hero on the back cover of *Beginner's Luck* by Dixie Browning:

> Specimen: Male; age 32; intense blue eyes hidden by thick glasses; gosh-awful beard; perpetual scowl; rear end worthy of the hall of fame.

Curiously enough, the glasses do not appear in the painting of the hero used on the cover. To compensate for his slight flaws, the author makes her hero a bona fide scientific genius. He is also marvellously athletic, and the first time the heroine sees him he is wielding an axe. He isn't wearing his glasses and has to come close to her, axe held high, to really see her. To her, he looks like a mad-eyed axe murderer.

So your hero does not have to conform to any stereotype but he does need to be larger than life, self-assured and successful, and definitely sexy. The romantic hero is a fantasy lover, the perfect mate every woman dreams of discovering, someone who can whisk her away from her everyday concerns. In keeping with the times, he may have come down to earth a little, but he should still represent an ideal. Not surprisingly, surveys conducted by Harlequin Mills & Boon show that most women definitely don't want to be married to a romantic hero, but they love meeting him at a safe distance in the pages of a book. So the fantasy remains as potent as ever.

Internal profile

(Create one for each of your main characters)

Name
Any nicknames and why
Special talents
Religion or beliefs
If none, reason for this
Own best trait
Own worst failing
Proudest moment in life so far
Biggest regret so far
Attitude towards money and why
Attitude towards the opposite sex and why
Most influential person in character's life
Goals and aspirations
This year, character wants?
Medium-term goals

Life's ambition and why
Character's biggest secret

Character questionnaire

Author   **Character (answers)**

What is your name?
What do you want?
Why do you want it?
What action will you take
   to achieve it?

Memory reveals character

As the examples illustrate, the best way to reveal character is through action and dialogue. You should avoid having long pages of internal monologue (when the character is thinking about her past), as this slows down the story. The heroine can have brief memories which establish her emotional motivation. If a longer reminiscence is needed to explain what is happening in the present, it may be better treated as a *flashback*, a fully dramatised scene from the past, complete with dialogue and narrative, just as she remembers it happening. Both memories and flashbacks should be used sparingly.

A memory can be as brief as one sentence, or a few paragraphs long. It can be used to fill gaps in time which would be tedious if dealt with in chronological order, as in this scene from *Centrefold*. The heroine, Danni, has reluctantly agreed to take her twin sister's place on a modelling assignment. Danni is a journalist with no modelling experience. I wanted to jump from Trina asking Danni the favour, to Danni on her way to the assignment, so I described the intervening weekend through Danni's thoughts:

Trina's last bit of advice was still ringing in Danni's ears as she prepared to leave for the photographic assignment. Her only consolation was how much happier Trina had looked when she left last night for her short vacation.

They had worked all weekend to turn Danni from a journalist into something approaching a model, and although Trina swore the transformation was complete, Danni still felt horribly unsure. Only the sight of her twin's face and listless demeanour had spurred her to go through with this. Trina really looked as if she needed the break, and she had been pathetically grateful when she'd left last night.

Memory also plays a large part in establishing the strength of the heroine's feelings for the hero. The fact that he stays so much in her mind shows just how much impact he has had on her, even if it wasn't all good at the time. Later, she will see that this was the foundation of the love they have come to share. In *Centrefold*, Danni meets the hero, Rowan Traynor, when he is working under pressure and not at his best. At first she doesn't realise that he has mistaken her for her twin, as she is unaware that he knows Trina. However, he does haunt her thoughts:

> To her astonishment, Danni found that she could remember every line of the man's disturbingly attractive face, down to the blue-black hair and chisel-shaped sideburns. If she admitted as much, Trina would have her paired off in no time, so she kept her thoughts to herself.

This example illustrates the importance of showing your characters' motivations instead of merely telling the reader about them. I could have said that Rowan Traynor haunted Danni's thoughts for the rest of the weekend.

Instead, I showed her fighting the memory and thinking of him in spite of herself.

Before you use flashes of memory or longer reminiscences, be sure that the memory has a direct bearing on the present. This makes it easier to decide what to include and what to leave out. How Trina prepares Danni to substitute as a fashion model has a direct bearing on Danni's actions in the story's present. But there is no need to detail how they spent the weekend, where or with whom.

So that the reader understands why Danni agreed to take Trina's place against her better judgment, I provide another flash of memory:

'Have you seen a doctor?'

Trina nodded. 'He says there's a virus going around. It wouldn't worry most people, but with my lungs . . .' Her voice trailed off.

Danni knew she was trapped. How could she let Trina undertake an assignment which might injure her health, when she was responsible for the scar tissue clouding her twin's lungs?

If only they hadn't gone sailing on their sixteenth birthday. But they had, and a swinging boom had knocked Danni overboard, stunning her as she sank like a stone. Suffering from a cold, Trina had dived repeatedly until she found Danni and brought her to shore, saving her life. Apart from a headache, Danni had suffered no ill effects, but Trina's cold had turned to pneumonia. Her recovery had required months of rest and treatment, and had left her with scarred lungs so she was prey to every chest infection going.

All because of me, Danni remembered. How did one repay a debt like that? 'Very well, I'll do it,' she said. All the same, she knew she had been manipulated by Trina, and wondered how many more times she would be called upon to repay her twin for saving her life.

In less than half a page, I establish why Danni is putty in Trina's hands, making her actions believable and sympathetic.

Note that Danni doesn't think at all about the twins' early lives. We don't learn whether they dressed alike as children, or anything else about their shared childhood. Having Danni think about any of this would slow down the story. The only information about her childhood which we need to know is the part affecting her actions now.

Flashbacks

A backward movement in the plot, during which the characters relive a complete scene from the past, is called a 'flashback'. It differs from a memory in that it includes dialogue and narrative: the character recalls the scene as if reliving it. Flashbacks are risky. The essence of good storytelling is to make the reader want to know what happens next, so an excursion into the past can slow down the story. But it may be unavoidable if the reader is to understand the character's actions in the story's present.

Barbara Taylor Bradford's *A Woman of Substance* is told almost entirely in flashback. It opens with the heroine, Emma Harte, arranging her business affairs to thwart her scheming offspring. As she makes her plans, she recalls how she came to be where she is. Her life story is told in a book-long flashback. By the time the book returns to Emma in the present, we understand what motivates her now. As an impoverished woman, she was betrayed by a rich lover and vowed to rise to a position of power to get her revenge. The unhappy love affair of her youth was the motivation for her success.

Deciding when to use a flashback will depend on the needs of the story. Flashbacks should only be used when the event being replayed has a direct bearing on the present. They should never be used to impart huge slabs of information about the characters when the information would be better introduced a little at a time. As Geoffrey Ashe says, 'You cannot afford to linger in paragraphs of description or reflection that take [the story] no further.'

In *Make Every Word Count*, Gary Provost says, 'At some level, the reader is always asking, "Why are you telling me this?" and if he doesn't understand why, he'll create an answer or lose his bearings. In either case, you lose his attention and your writing doesn't work.'

When a flashback is needed, it should be introduced by a natural trigger. The character's memory will be stirred by something. Think about what triggers your own memory—the sights, sounds and scents which transport you in mind to an earlier time or place. The taste of grape-fruit juice reminds me of journeying to Australia as a child aboard a migrant ship. It was the first time I had tasted grapefruit juice and the association is strong to this day. Music is another common trigger.

In *Centrefold*, it is the sight of models at work that reminds Danni why she is out looking for a job:

> Danni regarded the shivering models with sympathy. As a journalist, she had never envied the girls on the other side of the camera, knowing that their work was not as easy or glamorous as it appeared. Her sister's career was proof of that.

As she thought of Trina, a fresh wave of gloom clouded Danni's normally vivacious features. Much as she hated to admit it, it was largely because of Trina that Danni was job-hunting today.

As assistant editor of an influential investment magazine, she had thought she was secure for the foreseeable future. But, one week ago, everything had changed . . .

This is where we go into the flashback:

She had known something was wrong as soon as she arrived at her office, and sensed the tension in the air. 'It's Trina again, isn't it?' she asked the editor, Ray Conreid, when he summoned her to his office.

He frowned. 'I'm afraid so. Look, I know you two can't help looking so much alike, but sometimes I wish you were more like chalk and cheese, then I wouldn't be in the dilemma I'm in right now.'

'What's the matter?' she asked resignedly.

'It's the publisher. Mrs Philmont is such a stickler for the proprieties, as you know, and she does own this magazine. Well, she just found out about your sister's latest escapade, and she read the riot act to me on the phone this morning.'

'Surely you told her it wasn't me in the magazine?'

'I told her repeatedly. She says that isn't the point. The fact is, the subscribers *think* it's you, and they aren't going to give much credence to investment advice written by a . . . a nude centrefold.'

'So she told you to fire me, is that it?'

'I told her how unfair it was.'

Danni's eyes flashed fire. 'Then I'll save you the trouble, Ray, I'll resign as of this morning.'

Ray tried unsuccessfully to mask his relief. 'You needn't resign. This will probably blow over soon.'

'But not soon enough for Mrs Philmont. Don't worry, Ray, I've been thinking of changing jobs anyway. So you go ahead and tell Mrs P. that you did your duty. I'll be fine, honestly.'

'It still seems unfair,' he grumbled, but she noticed that he didn't try to make her change her mind. He offered her a fortnight's salary in lieu of notice, and wished her well, even as he ushered her out of his office.

With the decision made she felt strangely relieved. She had been tiring of the financial scene, but hadn't done anything about it. Now the decision had been made for her and she was almost glad. She was only sorry that she had just taken her annual holidays. The extra cash would have given her more time to look around. But at least she would have two weeks' pay in hand.

Three hours later, having cleaned out her desk and briefed the other journalists on the stories she'd been covering, she walked out of the office into unemployment.

Monarch Magazine was her third interview this week. She preferred not to think about the first two. Surely not everyone in Sydney thought she was this month's centrefold girl? The first two editors who had interviewed her evidently did, and their suggestive comments had warned her what to expect if she went to work for them. She hoped that today's interview would concentrate more on her writing skills and less on her supposed physical charms.

With an effort, she focused her attention on the scene in front of her. She could only see the photographer in silhouette but he was tall and powerfully built. He was also a perfectionist, judging by the way he was ordering the models around.

Like this one, most flashbacks come full circle, back to the event which triggered them—in this case, the sight of the models working with the photographer.

This flashback serves two purposes. It explains why Danni is out of a job—her publisher was outraged by the link between her highbrow financial journal and a centrefold model; and it shows that Danni is having a hard time finding a job. No matter how strenuously she denies it, people insist on thinking she's the one in the centrefold. So when Trina asks her to take over the modelling job, she has plenty of motivation for accepting it. We know that she needs the income to keep afloat, and since everyone thinks she's a model anyway, why not profit by it? I show only as much of her previous career as is needed to make these motives clear.

Flashbacks should be used only where absolutely necessary to explain the character's emotional motivation. Few things irritate readers more than a story which begins on an effective hook, grabs your attention, then trips off into the past. Recently, I read a draft of a science fiction novel in which a character announces an impending global catastrophe, then drifts into a reverie about how different the world is from the one he knew in childhood. Apart from having no bearing on the character's emotional motivation in the present, this reminiscence came at the wrong time. The flashback should occur when the character is in a position to reflect at length. When someone is driving a getaway car or saving the world, they have no time to stop and reminisce. Nor should they do so in the middle of a conversation with another character. What is that character doing in the meantime? Instead, pick a quiet moment when the character might logically have time to think about the past and its effect on her present.

You can see the importance of thoroughly researching your character's past. Building an inner profile of her life reveals which past events are likely to motivate her behaviour in the story's present. Working out these details before you begin writing saves much wasted time and energy, as well as giving your characters the kind of depth and dimension that editors seek so avidly.

Character checklist

- ♥ Are your characters believable, with pasts, futures, hopes and dreams? Based on this history, will the reader understand why they behave as they do (their motivation)?
- ♥ Have you made each character well-rounded, with weaknesses as well as strengths, shown through their actions?
- ♥ Have you chosen names which suit the characters? Try saying them aloud as a test. If she marries and changes her name, will her married name sound attractive?
- ♥ Have you given major and minor characters sufficiently different names to avoid confusion between them?
- ♥ Are character descriptions given in sensuous, original words? Are they woven in between action and dialogue?
- ♥ Do we meet the hero as early as possible and share the heroine's reaction to him, filtered through her senses?
- ♥ Is it clear why she can't give in to the attraction she feels?
- ♥ Is the hero a man the reader could fall in love with? If he's arrogant and strong, are his reasons made clear as the story progresses?

♥ If they make love, are both characters well motivated? Both should be willing participants even if they have misgivings.

♥ Does the reader share the characters' experiences through your use of viewpoint and original, sensuous words, phrases and dialogue?

♥ If there are love scenes, are they given their proper length and weight?

♥ Do you show how the characters change, what they've learned and what they've gained by the end of the book?

4
Viewpoint

ow many times have you heard the expression 'It's all in how you look at it' or 'One man's meat is another man's poison'? Both phrases assert the importance of viewpoint—the position from which one views an object or situation. In fiction, the viewpoint character is the one through whose eyes the reader experiences the events of the story. For many years, the viewpoint character was always the heroine, described in tip sheets as 'the gateway through which the reader enters the story'.

While use of viewpoint in romance novels has become a lot more flexible over time, the writer's job is still to create this gateway, enabling readers to imagine themselves as the lead character. These days most publishers encourage you to explore the hero's viewpoint as well as the heroine's. In a short category novel, this will be all you have room to do. In longer romance novels of 80 000 words or more, you may well have three or more viewpoint characters, although the main focus will still be on the hero and heroine.

There are many categories and subcategories of viewpoint and whole books have been written about the subject, but the main types which concern romance writers are:

- ♥ omniscient (godlike)
- ♥ first person (I did this or that)
- ♥ third person subjective (she did such-and-such)
- ♥ multiple viewpoint.

Omniscient

In omniscient viewpoint, the writer views all the characters from godlike heights and can step freely into any character's mind. The reader does not identify closely with any one character. This is why omniscient viewpoint isn't commonly used in romance novels. It makes it all too obvious that the writer is telling a story, harking back to the Victorian era when a writer could address the audience directly with expressions such as 'and now, dear reader . . .' Few modern writers would go this far, but it isn't unusual to come across phrases such as 'had she but known' or 'in a short time, she would discover . . .' The author is sharing information the viewpoint character doesn't have.

Phrases such as those given imply omniscience and take readers outside the viewpoint character, reminding them that they are reading a work of fiction.

A frequent mistake found in new writers' love scenes is slipping from 'he' or 'she' into 'they' to describe the action, possibly out of a disinclination to explore too deeply the powerful emotions the characters are experiencing. If you find yourself doing this, go back and rewrite the scene so we experience it through the viewpoint of either participant.

There is one valid use of omniscient viewpoint in romance writing, and that is to set the scene before we slip into the viewpoint character.

First person

This is easily recognised because the storyteller is 'I' and the reader is asked to take this role throughout the book. Although the reader participates vicariously in the events of the story, the writer is restricted to the events in which 'I' takes part. We cannot write about anything that happens when the viewpoint character is not present, when she is asleep or unconscious, for example.

Until recently, few romance novels were written in first person; however, books in the chick lit sub-genre frequently employ this viewpoint. *City Girl in Training* by Liz Fielding was one of the first category romance novels to be published in first person.

In first person, it is difficult to describe the heroine in flattering terms without making her sound vain. The opening paragraph of *Ask Me No Questions* was originally written from the viewpoint of Richard Bligh, the heroine's fiancé. You can see how awkward it sounds rewritten in the first person:

> Richard Bligh gazed affectionately at me, obviously delighted by the sight of my smooth, honey-coloured hair and large mahogany eyes set in almost translucent skin.

There are ways around the problem of showing your heroine in first person without making her sound vain. One is to have another character observe the viewpoint character and comment on her attractiveness:

> 'Do you think Richard really loves me?' I asked Sandra.
> She paused, half in and half out of the bridesmaid's dress she was trying on. 'Are you kidding? I've heard the

things he says to you. "You have the smoothest, honey-coloured hair and your skin is like fragile china," ' she mimicked Richard's admiring tones.

I threw a pillow at her and missed. 'Stop it. You know looks aren't everything.'

Another way is to have the heroine describe herself in self-deprecating terms, a hallmark of chick lit. In *City Girl in Training,* Liz Fielding's heroine is doing a quiz in a magazine, and learns that her score makes her 'a mouse':

I was too easygoing. Too undemanding. My expectations were so low they barely registered. I picked up my cheese sandwich and then put it down again quickly. Cheese. A mouse *would* choose a cheese sandwich.

I should be wearing designer label jeans with high heels, instead of an old pair that had once belonged to the last of my brothers to leave home—shortened to fit my pathetically short legs—with a pair of cheap trainers I'd bought from the market. (I was saving up to get married, okay?)

I should have had my nails professionally manicured. I should at least have painted them with something more exciting than the pale pink nail polish I'd borrowed from my mother.

An advantage of writing in first person is the ring of truth it carries, creating the impression that the story is being told by someone who actually experienced the events described.

Third person subjective

This is the most common viewpoint used in romance writing, and the easiest for a new writer to handle. Although third person is used—she said, she did, etc.—all the events and descriptions in the story are filtered through the mind and senses of the viewpoint character. This scene from *The Monarch's Son* is written from the third person subjective viewpoint. The setting is described as it is perceived by the heroine, Allie Carter:

Allie had seen enough of the royal residence to know that the rambling granite villa could easily provide the set for a movie based on a Jane Austen novel. But this was the first function she had attended here, and the grandeur of the Painted Salon was breathtaking.

The vast room took its name from a magnificent mural by a famous French artist that dominated the longest wall. The painting echoed the splendid ocean view the villa enjoyed from two sides. It was so realistic that Allie was tempted to try stepping through it to the seascape beyond to escape the curious eyes of the sixty or so other guests.

She couldn't speak more than a few words of the Carramer language, but she knew enough to recognize the word for Australian, and her own name, hovering on dozens of lips. Most of the glances directed at her were openly friendly and curious, but a handful were downright hostile, notably from a couple of older women chaperoning younger clones of themselves.

Mothers hoping Lorne would look favourably on their daughters? Their furious looks almost made Allie laugh aloud. Not only was she no threat to their ambitions, she didn't even want to be. If they only knew, Lorne had probably elected her as his escort because she was the only single woman in the room with no designs on him.

Not only do we see the Painted Salon as Allie sees it, but we also share her awareness of the impression she is making, gleaned from the reactions of the other guests. Again, once you have chosen third person narration, your viewpoint character cannot know anything other than their own thoughts and observations, or be aware of facts which they haven't read, heard from someone or learned from some other source. Allie's suspicion, phrased as a question in her mind, that the other women see her as a rival for their daughters, and her conclusion that Lorne 'probably' chose her because she had no designs on him, is as much as the author can share with us while remaining in Allie's viewpoint.

Multiple viewpoint

Multiple viewpoint, where several viewpoint characters are used to tell a story, is found more often in longer works such as single-title romances and mainstream novels. In longer novels, it enables the author to show scenes where the main viewpoint character is not present, such as the Civil War scenes in *Gone With the Wind* (Mitchell).

No matter how many viewpoint characters are used, one viewpoint character at a time should remain dominant. Brief switches in viewpoint, usually to a minor character, can be used to show the heroine through the eyes of another person. *Tasmanian Devil* is told through the eyes of the heroine, Evelyn Consett. However, in the opening scene, when she is being ferried to the island where she plans to spend a month fending for herself, I switch briefly to the viewpoint of the skipper, Ned Freils. I wanted to foreshadow what a tough time Evelyn was in for. Since she couldn't know this ahead of time, I used Ned's viewpoint:

Watching her, Ned smiled indulgently. She might think this was a great adventure, but she was in for a shock when reality caught up with her. Here, there were no servants or cooks, just the barest amenities—and a few surprises as well.

He schooled his features into a mask of composure. He shouldn't laugh. This was going to be harder than she imagined, and he hoped she wouldn't find it too daunting. For all her privileges, she was basically a nice kid—a lot like his own daughter, he realised. Except that at twenty-four, Judy was now married with a baby. Their lives were hardly comparable.

With the skill of long practice, he steered the thirty-footer into the shallows of a small bay which ended in a rough timber jetty. They were soon tied up and he began offloading the supplies: 'Would you like a hand to get these up to the cottage?'

She shook her head. She didn't want Ned telling her father that she couldn't even carry her own supplies. In fact, her heart sank at the sight of so many boxes to be carried to the cottage but she kept her voice light. 'I can manage. I've got plenty of time.'

The first two paragraphs are in Ned's viewpoint, giving us his view of Evelyn and softening our impression of her as a spoilt heiress. Her 'niceness' would be awkward if shown through her eyes.

To smooth the transition from Ned's viewpoint back to Evelyn's, I introduced a neutral paragraph which could be in either viewpoint, describing something they are both experiencing. The next paragraph is back in Evelyn's viewpoint, where we remain for the rest of the book.

Viewpoint as a writing tool

Publishers' tip sheets usually indicate which viewpoint they prefer for a particular imprint. Chick lit and mainstream novels can vary from first person to third, and even include a combination of viewpoints. Almost all short romance novels are written at least partially from the hero's viewpoint, some entirely so, and publishers are increasingly experimenting with first person narration. For a new writer, it may be easier to stick to the third person and only switch between viewpoint characters with care and full awareness that you have done so.

In the main you would switch to another viewpoint when something is gained by this, such as imparting new information which the heroine can't know. The Civil War scenes in *Gone With the Wind* are good examples. Scarlett wasn't a participant, and to have someone tell her what went on would have taken too long, so the author switched viewpoints for those scenes. However many viewpoints you decide to use, the changes should be smooth and unobtrusive to avoid jarring the reader. Soon, we'll look at some ways to switch viewpoint effectively.

If you've never consciously tried to write in viewpoint before, you may find it difficult to express everyday emotions from within a character's mind and body. Try catching yourself in various emotional states, and make notes. It may sound awkward, but it works. Next time you're exhausted, for example, think about the physical signals your body sends to your brain. Are your feet hot and blistered? Is perspiration trickling down between your shoulderblades? Does the blood throb in your temples and your hair lie in limp strands across your forehead? By including specific telling details like these, you make the reader aware of every nuance of the viewpoint character's emotional state.

Although you are writing that 'he' or 'she' did such-and-such, the details must be filtered through the senses of the viewpoint character. This helps you to avoid making basic mistakes such as having characters see themselves. Viewpoint characters spend so much time in front of mirrors and store windows because it's the only way they can observe their outward appearance while in viewpoint. We cannot see our own face turn red, for example:

> Susan's anger reached boiling point. Her face turned red and the veins in her neck stood out.

This is written as if Susan were being seen from the outside. In viewpoint, however, it should focus on her *internal* responses:

> Susan felt her temperature start to rise. Her skin burned with the rush of blood to her face and she felt the veins in her neck tighten with the effort of keeping her anger in check.

Always be aware of whose viewpoint you are using. If it is that of the heroine, for example, is the following passage in or out of her viewpoint?

> Susan felt genuinely sorry for the boy, who now cowered in a corner, his small hands clammy with fear.

It is out of viewpoint because Susan cannot look at another character and feel his clammy hands. She can guess that he is afraid, though, from the perspiration she sees beading his face and the trembling she observes in his limbs.

Your viewpoint character can assume, imagine or guess how another character feels, just as you do in everyday life, from the outward signs. Thus, you would write, 'The boy's silence told Susan that he was frightened' not 'Susan knew the boy was frightened'.

Attention to these details is essential. Readers may not be able to pinpoint what bothers them about your story but they will be irritated all the same.

Expressing viewpoint

The use of viewpoint becomes less mysterious when you think about how you come by your own awareness of the world. You only know what goes on in other people's lives when they choose to tell you. Likewise, you cannot know another person's thoughts, although you can guess what they're thinking from facial expressions, gestures and comments. Exponents of body language, say that a man who keeps adjusting his tie may not be telling the truth. On the other hand, his tie may be too tight! So it is with first, third or multiple viewpoints. The reader can only share what the viewpoint character observes, learns about or is told.

There are several ways to keep narrative passages in viewpoint. One is to use language that the viewpoint character would use. Which of these sounds as if it is in the hero's viewpoint?

> He knew damned well what was going on. Her evasiveness and refusal to explain where she'd been meant she was still seeing someone else in spite of her promises.
>
> He was convinced of what had occurred. Failing to keep her promise, she had taken up with another man.

Without any other narrative landmarks, the language itself suggests that the hero is speaking in the first example. In the second, it could be anyone.

Another device is to use names as the character would use them. For example, the heroine of *The Prince and the Marriage Pact* is Annegret West. She thinks of herself as Annegret. To her mother, she is Greta. Using different forms of a name can indicate the character's relationship with other people, provided you make it clear that they are all the same person:

> 'Greta dear?'
> At the sound of her nickname, Annegret looked up.
> 'Yes, mother?'

One way to test whether you are anchored firmly in viewpoint is to write a few paragraphs, then read them aloud, substituting 'I' for 'she' with any other small grammatical changes required. The passage should sound plausible. If not, there may be places where you are slipping out of viewpoint. This paragraph from *Tasmanian Devil* shows what I mean. As published, it reads:

> Although the day was mild, Evelyn's throat was arid by the time she retraced her steps to her cottage. She blamed her agitated mood on her encounter with Dane Balkan. He had a nerve, expecting her to leave her own island to him.

In the test version, you would read it aloud like this:

> Although the day was mild, my throat was arid by the time I retraced my steps to my cottage. I blamed my agitated

mood on my encounter with Dane Balkan. He had a nerve, expecting me to leave my own island to him.

Nothing in the altered passage is physically impossible. I can feel my throat becoming dry, I can blame my mood on an external event, and I can plausibly react as described. Having done the test, I can go back to writing in third person again.

Another way to bring the reader closer to your viewpoint character is by deleting as many 'tags' as possible, such as 'she thought' and 'she wondered'. You will probably write them into your first draft but many can be deleted at the editing stage. Names can also be replaced by pronouns at this stage. Most writers use the characters' names too often in first drafts. The eye skips over pronouns such as 'she' and 'her', so names should be replaced with pronouns as much as possible without disorienting the reader. This removes yet another barrier between the reader and your story.

Which viewpoint should you use?

Most romances are told primarily from the heroine's viewpoint, although use of the hero's viewpoint is also common. In shorter romances, alternative viewpoints can be used to provide suspense where the heroine doesn't know some crucial fact.

A switch to another viewpoint can also help the reader understand that character's motivations. For example, in *Royal Spy* Gage Weston is in love with Princess Nadia Kamal, but his life is in imminent danger. He has to get her away from him without delay:

It took almost more willpower than he possessed not to take her in his arms, but he dared not. Not if his plan to get her away safely was to have any chance of success. If she had the slightest notion of the danger facing him, he was sure she would refuse to budge. That left him only one option. Somehow he had to convince her that she had been no more than a memorable one-night stand to him.

Without going into Gage's viewpoint, we might believe as Nadia does, that he is as dishonourable as his words suggest, and he would lose reader sympathy. Instead, his behaviour is seen as heroic, because we understand the sacrifice he is making on her account.

When writing 'in viewpoint', you should allow the reader to see as much as possible through the viewpoint character's eyes and senses. This helps you to decide which descriptions to include and which to leave out. If the heroine is the viewpoint character and she enters a room, describe only the features which she would naturally notice. In *Tasmanian Devil*, Evelyn visits Dane Balkan's cottage for the first time. Filtering the description through her senses means it is not necessary to describe every detail, only those she sees and her reactions to them:

It was the first time she'd been inside the other dwelling and she was surprised at how different it was from her cabin.

It was built from local stone with an iron roof and vine-shaded back veranda. Tree trunks washed the same pale green as the house served as unusual supports for the rainwater tank at one side.

The front door opened on to a large room with a fireplace at one end. The floor was made of thick boards butted tightly together, with a scattering of rugs for warmth. Overhead she noticed a large trapdoor which presumably led to a loft bedroom similar to her own.

A romance heroine would notice the way to the bedroom. By highlighting this aspect of her awareness, I reinforce her feelings for the hero. Also, note the use of the word 'presumably'. Since this is her first visit to the cabin, she can only guess that the trapdoor leads to a bedroom. She cannot know.

Her reactions are as important as the description. Is she impressed, overwhelmed at the Spartan decor, dismayed at what she's got herself into? Her state of mind will have a bearing on what she notices. The same applies to descriptions of what your characters are wearing. There is no need to describe every seam and button. Filtering the description through the heroine's senses will help you to decide which details to mention. When Evelyn is dressing to have dinner with Dane, I include only a few telling details:

> Now she dressed with care in a taupe linen trouser suit which didn't look too out of place in the simple surroundings. At her throat she knotted a Bill Blass scarf, then fixed huge gold hoops to her ears. After seeing the way Dane dressed, she wondered if she was overdressed, but it was the closest her wardrobe came to rustic simplicity.

It would have been out of character to have her dressing in jeans and T-shirt, since this is her first attempt at roughing it. The beginning of her character change is hinted at in her concern that she might be overdressed, but for Evelyn Consett, she *is* casually dressed. Keeping your character's background in mind will remind you to infuse this kind of detail into the scene. You should ask yourself repeatedly: Is this action or description in character for the person I have created? If I were she, what would I notice when I walked into the hero's home? Putting yourself figuratively into the character's shoes is the key to writing successfully in viewpoint.

How to switch viewpoints

In one of the examples above, when my heroine arrives on her island, we see her first through the eyes of the ferry skipper then move into her viewpoint. Note how his thoughts and feelings differ from those of the heroine, because each viewpoint character's awareness of their surroundings is different.

If you have been writing in the heroine's viewpoint then switch to that of the hero and he is taller than she, he will be looking down at her, where previously we looked up at him from her eye level. You should always change viewpoints consciously and stay with one viewpoint character at a time for several paragraphs or pages, to avoid disorienting your reader. Don't switch viewpoints within a paragraph, a bad habit known as 'head-hopping'. To help in reader identification, I prefer to write love scenes mainly from the heroine's point of view, switching into the hero's viewpoint to show his feelings for the heroine.

How do you bring about a change in viewpoint? In *Sapphire Nights*, I used several methods. Switching at a chapter break is one of the easiest for the reader to follow. At the end of the first chapter I was writing in the heroine's viewpoint:

As the admission slipped out, she felt the colour creeping up her neck and face. Damn! Now she had blown her cover story of being Mitchell Fraser's long-time secretary.

Rex studied her curiously. 'I see.' Gently but firmly he took the spoon from her fingers and set it down, then tilted her face towards him. 'You've already said more than you meant to. So how about telling me the rest, starting with who you really are.'

I prepare the reader for a switch by focusing on Rex in the last paragraph, although we are still in the heroine's viewpoint. (Dialogue, of course, is written in the viewpoint of the person speaking.) The next chapter opens in Rex's viewpoint:

As soon as he saw her face fall, Rex regretted forcing the issue so soon. Now he'd frightened her off with his confounded suspicions. She was probably just an acting hopeful Mitch had installed here, planning to make her his mistress eventually.

Describing the heroine's facial expression from Rex's vantage point is a signal that we have changed viewpoint. Note also the different uses of the heroine's father's name. In her mind, he is 'Mitchell Fraser'. To Rex, an old friend of her father's, he is 'Mitch'.

A time change is another way to indicate a change in viewpoint:

She was impossible, a typical spoiled, self-centred movie brat, he thought as he headed for his room. He didn't even trust himself to say goodnight, far less respond to her taunt.

Four lines of space indicates a switch in time and viewpoint.

> Why did it have to be Rex Marron who turned up here now? Belle wondered as she got ready for bed. Try as she might to ignore it, the vestiges of her teenage crush on him were still there, and her stomach muscles cramped in response to the sounds coming from the guest room nearby.

The link between 'to say goodnight' and 'as she got ready for bed' alerts the reader to the fact that some time has passed. If a chapter break or time change is unsuitable, three asterisks can indicate a change of viewpoint within a scene:

> He lifted his body a fraction and she used the moment to wriggle out from under him and strike out for the far side of the pool where she hoisted herself up onto the coping. 'Whoever called you Mister Nice Guy didn't know what they were talking about,' she threw at him as she stood up. 'Now I can see why Laine Grosvener walked out on you.'
>
> *   *   *
>
> He watched as she stalked away, annoyance in every line of her body. He wished some of his critics who said he couldn't act his way out of a paper bag had been there to witness the scene.
>
> Coming on to Belle when he had no intention of following through was one of the toughest things he'd ever done.

Whatever method you use to bring about a switch in viewpoint, you should be aware of whose viewpoint you're using, so you limit the character's thoughts and experiences to what they can glean through their senses. Properly handled, viewpoint is one of the most powerful writing tools at your disposal. It can take the reader into the story so they live it vicariously, instead of only reading about it.

Viewpoint checklist

- ♥ Have you checked the publisher's tip sheet when deciding whether to use single or multiple viewpoint?
- ♥ If you shift viewpoint, can you pinpoint the shift? Is it intentional, and is the transition smooth and easy to follow?
- ♥ If using more than one viewpoint, do you switch for good reasons and make your transitions carefully at opportune moments, such as at the end of a scene or chapter?
- ♥ If using omniscient (godlike) viewpoint to set a scene, do you switch to a viewpoint character quickly and smoothly?
- ♥ When using the hero's viewpoint, do you use the switch to reveal his character, show a different view of the heroine, and/or reveal information she doesn't have?
- ♥ Do you describe people, clothing and settings in viewpoint—that is, filtered through the eyes and senses of the viewpoint character so the reader sees and feels what that character sees and feels?
- ♥ In narrative passages, do you use the language of the viewpoint character so we share their thoughts first-hand?

♥ Do you use names as the characters would use them when they refer to each other or think of themselves? Have you explained any nicknames through references in the narrative?

♥ Do you slip out of the viewpoint at any time, by describing how another character feels when the viewpoint character cannot know; or by describing your viewpoint character from the outside? Physical descriptions should be given in such a way that the character can see them, say, in a mirror.

♥ When deliberately switching viewpoints, do you prepare the reader by the words you use? If not, do you indicate the change by a switch in time, a four-line space break or three asterisks between one viewpoint and the next?

5

Dialogue

We live in an electronic age, trained by television, films and DVDs to absorb information through what the characters say. As a result, novels now contain far more dialogue than narrative. Recently, I watched someone browsing in a bookstore, opening book after book and flipping through the pages. Several volumes later, she chose one and took it to the cash register. Intrigued, I asked her how she had made her decision to buy. She explained, 'This one looks easy to read.'

Comparing the volumes she discarded with the one she chose revealed that her choice had short paragraphs, lots of white space and no daunting-looking slabs of narrative—in other words, lots of dialogue. Compare these two passages. This was not published:

> Tiredly, Nikki passed a hand over her eyes. Why couldn't Richard just accept that she no longer wanted to be engaged to him? Throwing threats back and forth wasn't going to do any good. But Matt stood up slowly and deliberately, anger in every line of his body, obviously determined to warn Richard off. His expression was ugly and she wondered if he would remember that Matt had been unable to make love to her when he caught them in bed together the other day.
>
> For a horrifying moment, Nikki thought that Matt was going to hit Richard. He was asking for it, but he wasn't

fully in control of himself. Luckily Matt seemed to realise it and relaxed the hands he had balled into fists, ordering Richard to get out instead. But Richard took up a fighting stance and shadow-boxed close to Matt's face, challenging him to a fight.

This is the published version in *Ask Me No Questions*:

Tiredly, she passed a hand over her eyes. 'Talking like that won't do any good. I've told you how I feel. Why won't you accept it?'

Like a cobra coiling for the strike, Matt stood up slowly and deliberately. 'You heard Nikki. She just wants you to leave her alone.'

Richard's expression was ugly. 'And what does she want from you, what she couldn't get the other day because lover-boy couldn't deliver?'

So he *did* remember. For a horrifying moment, Nikki thought Matt was going to hit Richard. He was asking for it, but he wasn't fully in control of himself. Luckily, Matt seemed to realise it and relaxed the hands he had balled into fists. 'Get out of here,' he said coldly.

Richard took up a fighting stance and shadow-boxed close to Matt's face. 'Make me,' he challenged.

Apart from the actual words, the second version appears more interesting. It allows the characters to speak for themselves, so the reader learns what's going on first-hand, instead of being told by the writer.

Small talk is not dialogue. Writers' how-to books say that dialogue has to sound natural and unstilted, the way people really talk. But sounding natural and being natural are two different things.

In everyday speech, people speak ungrammatically, leaving sentences and thoughts unfinished. They ramble, stutter, talk over each other and seldom really hear the other person because they're busy rehearsing what they plan to say next. Dialogue as natural as this would never be published. If it were, who would want to read it?

Dialogue that sounds natural will contain contractions, 'I'll' instead of 'I will', and so on. The speaker's voice will fade away, leaving part of the words unspoken, and the speech will contain some of the natural rhythms of the speaker. But it will never be empty and meaningless, used simply to fill space.

Writers generally fall into two camps: narrative writers and dialogue writers. I am among the latter: I have to remind myself to balance dialogue with narrative because I'm not writing a script. I find dialogue far more interesting and pacy than narrative, and much more enjoyable to write. But what if your inclination goes the other way?

If you have to struggle to write dialogue, it may be because you're overlooking the work the dialogue has to do. Far from being idle chatter which breaks up the narrative, dialogue has to help tell the story. In an old audiocassette called *And Then He Kissed Her . . .*, Mills & Boon said that dialogue has to do five things:

♥ claim reader attention and set the story in motion
♥ allow the characters to reveal themselves
♥ provide information
♥ add pace and tension, create emotional mood
♥ move the story along.

Claim the reader's attention

I frequently start a chapter with a line of dialogue because it commands instant reader interest. In *Royal Spy,* chapter two opens with an exchange of dialogue between Princess Nadia and a doctor she secretly assists at a children's shelter, after her first meeting with Gage, whom she believes to be a diplomat.

> "Aren't you concerned that your British diplomat will blow the whistle on you at the palace?" the doctor asked as soon as the infirmary doors closed behind Gage.
>
> Nadia frowned. "He thinks I'm Tahani, the ladies' maid. As long as I stay out of his way when he presents his credentials at court, there's no reason for him to think I'm Princess Nadia."

If you're ever stricken with writer's block, I recommend starting with a line of dialogue. It immediately demands a response and the scene will soon start taking shape. Other examples of attention-getting openings are:

> 'What time did you say he was coming?'
> 'Oh no, not *him* again!'
> 'What on earth are you doing here?'
> 'I don't believe you.'
> 'Make me.'

These are just a few of many provocative lines you could use to get a scene moving. Once you get the idea, it's easy to think of similar lines of your own. If a scene seems to be bogged down in narrative, try to introduce another character and convey the same information in the form of dialogue.

Allow characters to reveal themselves

This is 'show, don't tell' again. What do we learn about Nikki, Richard and Matt in this scene from *Ask Me No Questions*?

> Without looking at Richard, Nikki scribbled down the room number Matt gave her. Luckily she already knew the address of the motel where he was staying. When she hung up, she found Richard looking at her in disgust. 'You're not actually going to him?'
>
> Her eyes begged for his understanding. 'Matt's ill. He needs me.'
>
> His expression was unrelenting. 'If he's ill, he needs a doctor. Why didn't he call one instead of bothering you?'
>
> 'I don't know why, but I can't just ignore him. He probably doesn't know many people in Sydney. I was the first person he thought of, most likely.'
>
> Richard didn't seem convinced. 'More likely it's just a ruse to lure you to his hotel room.'
>
> She hadn't thought of anything like that, but she dismissed such fanciful notions out of hand. 'Matt isn't like that.'

From the dialogue, would you conclude that Richard was caring and compassionate towards someone in trouble? Hardly! His attitude is the very opposite. He doesn't want anything to do with the problem.

What about Nikki's response? On the strength of a phone call, she's willing to drop everything and rush to Matt's aid. Not only is she a friend in need, it is also possible that she still cares about Matt (her ex-husband). She doesn't have a suspicious bone in her body, or Richard wouldn't have to suggest that the phone call could be a clever ruse. Without knowing anything else about the story, we learn a great deal about these three people, far more convincingly than if the author had tried to explain to us what they are like.

Impart information

As well as learning about the characters, the reader can learn more of the story through dialogue, reducing the need for long chunks of narrative and getting the information across with far less authorial intrusion. Continuing the scene from *Ask Me No Questions*, what does the reader learn of the story background as the dialogue goes on:

> 'Matt isn't like that.'
>
> Richard's brows came together. 'Oh? You know so much about him then?'
>
> 'I was married to him, for goodness' sake.'
>
> 'And now you're supposed to be marrying me,' he reminded her. Seeing her stricken expression, he relented slightly, 'I'm sorry. I'm not trying to force you to choose between us—I'm counting on the fact that you've already made your choice. I just don't like the way he's trying to exploit his past relationship with you.'

Narrative is unnecessary for the reader to learn that Nikki was once married to Matt and is now engaged to Richard. That all is not well with her new relationship is obvious from the lack of solidarity they demonstrate over Matt's illness. Again, you don't need to have read this particular book to glean a great deal of story background and character information from this conversation.

Add pace and tension, create mood

These are two of the most important jobs dialogue has to do. By itself, two people talking won't move the story along unless, as in the example above, the reader is given new information or a new slant on what they already know. Nikki's ambivalence towards Matt, shown in her dialogue, plants the suggestion that she may still be in love with him.

Pace is the sense of the story carrying the reader along so they are almost unaware of the words themselves, only of what they are telling them about these interesting people.

I always know I'm in trouble when my characters start being nice to each other. If they are truly in conflict, it shows in their dialogue. Listening to Nikki and Richard, you can almost sense the undercurrent of tension. Richard is afraid he may be losing her, and this is revealed by his defensive behaviour.

Another kind of tension can be generated in dialogue—sexual tension. The characters may not talk about their feelings but enough clues should be planted so the undercurrents are obvious to the reader, if not to the characters themselves:

[Nikki] was so preoccupied with trying to fasten the larger suitcase that she didn't hear the bedroom door open behind her.

'What the devil is going on here?'

She spun around, her heart hammering with shock, to find Matt standing in the doorway, his arms folded aggressively across his chest. His expression was grim.

'What does it look like? I'm packing to leave,' she said, trying to keep her voice steady.

'Just because I had to go away for twenty-four hours?' he asked incredulously.

She schooled her features into a carefree mask, adding a shrug of her shoulders for good measure. 'What's twenty-four hours after six years?'

This piece of dialogue operates on two levels. On one level, Nikki tells Matt she is leaving and that his absence had nothing to do with it. But underneath her careless words, the reader is made aware that she cares a great deal. That she is 'trying to keep her voice steady' and 'adding a shrug of her shoulders for good measure' signals the reader not to take her words at face value even if the hero does.

Move the story along

Dialogue should never be idle chatter. It should always serve one of the five purposes described here; preferably more than one. In the first scene from *Ask Me No Questions*, the dialogue is used to advance the story from Matt's telephone call telling Nikki that he is ill, to her overruling Richard's objections and going to Matt's side. This is what is meant by 'moving the story along'. At the end of the discussion, the story should have progressed from the point at which we came into it. Some action should be decided upon (or against, if this serves your story), or your characters should be better friends or worse enemies than they were when the conversation started. The best way to teach yourself how to do this is to read as many dialogue scenes as possible from published novels and note down where the characters are at the start of the scene and what progress has occurred by the end of the scene.

Long passages of unbroken dialogue can be as monotonous as unbroken narrative. When actors have lines to say, they are given what is called 'business' to occupy their hands and bodies. A few years ago, lighting a cigarette was a popular bit of business. These days, actors are more likely to busy themselves pouring a drink.

Whatever business you give your actors to do should have a bearing on the scene. Drinking coffee together is fine, provided the conversation is social. It can also be ironic, if the characters are in conflict. The chummy coffee scene is a useful counterpoint to a conversation which has undercurrents of hostility. In the scenes quoted above, some of the business includes Nikki scribbling down Matt's room number and hanging up the telephone. In the later scene, she is packing a suitcase. Both actions contribute to the tension in the scene, rather than simply filling in space between lines of dialogue. Gestures can also be used as business:

> Matt patted her arm reassuringly.
> Her eyes begged for his understanding.
> She schooled her features into a carefree mask, adding a shrug of her shoulders for good measure.

It helps to picture the scene in your mind, as if it were being projected on a movie screen. How are the characters placed when the scene opens? Perhaps one is seated and the other comes in through a door. What are they doing? Who speaks first? How does the second person react? What are they doing while they talk? Answering these questions will help you to integrate dialogue and narrative while achieving each of the five steps.

As one writer expressed it, 'All barks and no kisses can be very tedious.' Having your characters in conflict is well and good, and very necessary to hold the reader's interest. But this is a love story. At the same time as they are solving their problems, the characters must also be falling in love. This is difficult if they spend the entire book arguing. Your plot outline must provide for scenes which give the hero and heroine a chance to get to know each other.

In *Royal Spy*, the hero's skilful driving saves the heroine's life when their brakes fail while driving along a cliff road. In the aftermath of the shared trauma they become closer, eventually making love. Naturally, this harmony can't be allowed to go on for too long. Just when they are starting to make progress the lovers are separated by the man her father wants her to marry. It's a case of 'two steps forward, one step back'. Each time, they get a little closer to each other, so that by the end of the story it is perfectly natural for them to ride off into the sunset together.

Variety in dialogue

In real life, we don't all sound alike. Neither should your characters. Their background, education and personality should show in their speech patterns. If a character is foreign, there's no need to try to imitate an accent, which makes the dialogue hard to read. Instead, aim to provide a suggestion of an accent or dialect: 'It is—how you say in English?—a dog's dinner.'

In *Heir to Danger*, my heroine is from a European sheikdom, hiding out in Australia from an arranged marriage. Rather than endow her with a foreign accent, I sprinkled her speech with the occasional reminder: 'And you're—what do you call it?—holding a candle for him?'

Omit all unnecessary words in dialogue (although you will probably write them into your first draft and delete them later). These include words such as 'well', 'honestly', 'in fact', 'to be perfectly frank'—and similar expressions which pepper everyday speech but contribute nothing to good fiction writing.

Stated, averred or declared?

New writers have a strong aversion to the word 'said' and go to almost any lengths to avoid it. Every piece of dialogue will have a different tag. It will be 'stated', 'averred', 'declared', 'demanded', 'raged', 'whispered' ... but never 'said'. Dialogue tags like these can add variety, but when overused they draw attention to themselves and spoil reader identification. The eye glides over 'he said' and 'she said' to the point where we hardly notice they're there. Unless you have a valid reason for using a different tag, 'said' is almost always preferable.

With care, you can avoid many dialogue tags altogether. The examples given in this chapter show how to use gestures, facial expressions and movements in place of dialogue tags. As long as the reader always knows who's speaking, you can use whichever devices you prefer to identify a speaker. Be especially careful when two people of the same sex are conversing. Too many references to 'she' can become confusing. It's better occasionally to distinguish the characters by other means, such as 'The redhead got to her feet', 'The younger woman smiled'.

Avoid repeating information

Sometimes, an author uses dialogue to impart to the reader information which the speakers would already have. This is artificial and draws attention to itself:

'As you know, dear sister, Mum and Dad are on their second honeymoon on the Gold Coast and won't be back until next week.'

This is the author intruding, feeding lines to the characters. Putting yourself into viewpoint should help you overcome this problem. People do tell each other things they already know, but to make a point of their own:

'Trust you to take advantage of Mum and Dad's absence, dear sister. Some second honeymoon it will be if they come back and find you've sold all the family silver. If I were you I'd replace it before they get back on Friday.'

The same information is imparted to the reader, but in the viewpoint of the character speaking. She isn't just telling her sister something she already knows, she is adding to the information for her own purposes.

'She said angrily'

Originally, dialogue tags like this were a hallmark of the romance genre. Fortunately, higher editorial standards and increased competition mean that romance writing must be as polished as writing for any other medium. You can avoid the need for adverbs like 'angrily', 'crossly', 'cheerfully', and their stable mates, by making the dialogue speak for itself. In the example given, when Nikki tells Richard 'I was married to him, for goodness' sake', I don't need to add 'she said impatiently'. Her mood is clear from the words she uses. Similarly, when Matt asks 'What the devil is going on here?' there's no need to add 'he demanded furiously'. The speaker's mood is implicit in the dialogue. You may like to use adverb tags for variety, or if the spoken words alone do not indicate the mood of the speaker. Irony, where the speaker says one thing and means the opposite, is one such case. But avoid peppering your dialogue with tags to no good purpose.

Try to 'loosen up' when writing dialogue, especially in chick lit and single-title books where it's important for the characters to reflect contemporary thinking. In everyday life, people speak in half-sentences and use poor grammar and contractions. Your characters will sound more convincing if they don't speak perfect English unless, of course, this is part of their make-up. Allow your characters to interrupt each other and misinterpret one another's words, but make sure the reader understands what is going on. A character shouldn't break off in mid-sentence until the reader has the sense of what is being said.

If the speaker is the viewpoint character, it's perfectly in order to let the reader know what her state of mind is before she speaks. However, be careful not to slip out of viewpoint with phrases such as 'Her voice dropped. "What is he doing here?"' The speaker's voice cannot drop until she speaks. Also, avoid making your viewpoint character appear psychic. 'Lena went to the kitchen to make the coffee. "Black or white?" she called out.' How does the viewpoint character know Lena's intention is to make coffee until she speaks? This would be more correctly written as, 'Lena went to the kitchen and Susan heard the sounds of coffee being made. "Black or white?" came the voice from the kitchen.'

Dialogue presentation

Every publisher has its own house style for setting out a manuscript, including the dialogue. Studying its published works will indicate preferred spelling, whether dialogue is enclosed in single or double quotation marks, and similar housekeeping details. Generally, dialogue is placed within single quotes by British publishers, such as Harlequin Mills & Boon, and double quotes by American houses such as Silhouette. A good novel won't be rejected because you've used single quotes instead of double. But it makes sense to be as professional as you can in your presentation, coming as close to the publisher's preferred style as is practicable.

In general, when characters interrupt each other, the dialogue should end in a dash:

> 'But Julian, you said—'
> 'Dammit, Marie, I know what I said,' he interrupted.

If the speaker trails off without finishing what he or she was saying, use an ellipsis (three dots):

> 'Oh Julian, you're so . . .' Her voice faded as she tried to think of a suitable description.

If there is no dialogue tag such as 'he said' after the speech, finish with a full stop within the quotation marks.

> 'Dammit, Marie, I know what I said.'

Only use a comma where a dialogue tag follows the spoken words:

> 'Dammit, Marie, I know what I said,' he interrupted.

Or:

> He interrupted, 'Dammit, Marie, I know what I said.'

Or:

> 'Dammit, Marie,' he interrupted, 'I know what I said.'

Only one person should speak in each paragraph. All the dialogue, tags and narrative relating to that speech should be contained within the one paragraph. If the speech is a long one, however, you may break it up into two or more paragraphs. To indicate that the same person is still speaking, do not close the quotation at the end of the first paragraph. Open new quotation marks to start the second paragraph and close them at the end of the speech, like this:

> To her relief, he accepted her story. 'Then it's time you heard my side so you know what sort of a man Slade is. A few months before the robbery, I got a tip that there was some rainforest land for sale along the Whitsunday Coast.
>
> 'Sold off as a time-sharing resort, it would have been worth a fortune, and I could've bought it very cheaply. But the locals wanted it left as virgin bush, and there was an outcry when my plans became public.'

Finally, make your dialogue *romantic*. This doesn't mean peppering it with flowery phrases or lines such as 'How dare you!' How long is it since you heard anyone actually say that? Dialogue should paint a mental picture and add to the romantic atmosphere of your story.

Humour is also valuable. If the characters share a humorous moment, we can see them growing closer together. A little wit, a little gentle teasing, all add spice and sparks to your fictional relationship, just as they do to a real-life love affair. One of my favourite scenes comes near the end of *Inherit the Storm*. The hero, known as

'Way' Longstreet because his initials are W.A., has just proposed to the heroine:

> He started to kiss her again but she pushed him playfully away. 'If we're going to be married, shouldn't you tell me what your initials stand for?'
>
> 'You'll find out at the wedding ceremony,' he teased. 'Until then, you can call me darling.'
>
> 'Then I'll have to guess. How about "wonderful" and "adorable"?'
>
> He shook his head. 'Too romantic. Actually, it's "willing and able".'

And he proceeds to demonstrate how apt the names are. I never did explain what his initials stand for. In another scene from the same book, I had them sparring verbally while she is packing to leave. As fast as she puts things into a suitcase, he pulls them out and throws them around the room. Her underwear ends up hanging from a lightshade. Used appropriately, humour provides a welcome respite from conflict and sexual tension and makes the growing relationship even more convincing.

Dialogue checklist

- ♥ Do the characters each have a distinctive 'voice' in keeping with your characterisation of them?
- ♥ Does the dialogue sound natural without imitating the clumsiness of everyday speech?
- ♥ Does each piece of dialogue carry the story forward? Alternatively, does it get attention, reveal character or add pace and tension—preferably doing several jobs at once?

♥ If imparting information, do you keep dialogue in viewpoint so characters do not tell each other what they already know?

♥ Do your characters speak in clichés, or is their conversation fresh and sparkling with every unnecessary word omitted?

♥ Do your characters have interesting things to do while speaking, to break up the dialogue?

♥ Do characters talk to each other at every opportunity? Check to see whether any narrative passages can be rewritten to include dialogue.

♥ Have you eliminated all unnecessary dialogue tags ('he said', 'she murmured') without risking the reader losing track of who's speaking?

♥ Does the tone of the dialogue reveal the speaker's mood, eliminating the need for tags such as 'she said angrily'?

♥ Does your manuscript appear easy to read, with short paragraphs and 'tennis-match' dialogue, where the characters speak in turn rather than lecturing each other?

♥ Is the ending told mostly through dialogue, as the characters clear up any misunderstandings, review the doubts they had about each other and anticipate their future?

♥ Above all, is the dialogue *romantic*? Even when the characters are in conflict, is their growing love revealed by the way they speak to each other?

6
Plot and conflict

What is the story about? What happens next? These are questions that you want the reader to ask, so first you must be able to answer them yourself. This is where story structure, plot and conflict come in. Plot is almost always where the new writer starts, but with a romance novel so much of the plot is predetermined that you have more chance of writing an original story if you start with your characters.

The previous chapters show how to get to know your characters thoroughly. By following the steps, you will know what your characters are likely to want—their goals—and what actions they might take to achieve them. This should lead you directly into the beginnings of your plot, which you will then expand into an outline so you are ready to start writing the manuscript.

Editor Anne Gisonny calls a plot 'a tightly integrated series of scenes set in motion by some directing idea. Something like a line of dominoes falling one into the next.'

The heroine's goals will usually supply the directing idea. How the hero stands in the way of her goals provides the conflict. Without a sense of direction and conflict, the book can become a series of chance meetings and unplanned events where the characters argue endlessly before falling inexplicably in love on the last page.

Some editors say that the developing romance *is* the plot of a short novel, with the story itself as subplot. However you describe it, the story must support and illuminate the central love story. How the characters meet, what keeps them from giving in to the attraction they feel, and how they resolve their differences form the core of your book. Everything else is secondary.

As soon as the reader sets eyes on your hero and heroine, they know the characters will end up living happily ever after. Your job is to make them worry that this time the outcome could be different. Your plot must answer three questions:

- ♥ Why are the hero and heroine attracted to each other?
- ♥ What keeps them apart?
- ♥ How will they resolve the 'what'?

The first question will be answered by your character profiles, both internal and external. Initially, she will probably be attracted to his appearance. As they get to know one another, they will find in each other qualities worthy of their love.

The answer to the second question—what keeps them apart—is the body of your story. It provides the essential conflict without which there would be no need to keep reading. The conflict is the obstacle the characters must overcome before they can give in to the attraction they feel.

If it is to last for 50 000 to 100 000 words or more, the conflict needs to be stronger than mutual, unmotivated dislike or, worse still, a complete lack of communication. Too often, conflicts could be resolved if the parties simply talked to each other. Similarly, the conflict should not depend on something as slight as an overheard conversation or another woman lying to the heroine about her relationship with the hero. These days, some editors say that having your characters come from 'two different worlds' is not enough to keep them apart. The feeling is that two modern, reasonably intelligent people should be able to overcome such differences.

Other issues you should avoid in your plotting include: contrivances; coincidences; drugs and alcohol, unless very skilfully handled and appropriate for the line; international terrorism; abortion; racial conflict; and the Other Woman as the sole source of disagreement.

Some issues, such as abortion, can defeat the purpose of romance, which is escapist entertainment. Others, such as terrorism, while it may be an acceptable element in action–adventure romance lines, still require careful handling if they are not to overshadow the love story. The Other Woman is passé as the sole source of conflict because of changing times and an emphasis on women supporting rather than competing with each other.

This shows what a challenge the romance medium provides for a writer. So much has already been done that it's difficult to come up with a story which is fresh and original.

However, it can be done. The marriage of convenience was a new idea once. Look at some other overused plots and see how you can give them your own original twist. In *Boss of Yarrakina*, for example, my heroine is forced to marry the hero before her much-loved godmother will agree to have vital surgery. The heroine is a professional stuntwoman and hires an actor friend to perform the ceremony. They are never actually married. By the time she finds herself wishing they had been, it is too late.

Another much-used device is to give the heroine amnesia. Invariably, she wakes up alongside a stranger who swears he is her husband. In *Remember Me, My Love*, I gave the hero amnesia for a change. As a further twist, he flatly refuses to believe his wife when she tracks him down. Her efforts to reawaken their love form the plot of the book.

There are many ways to give old ideas new twists. Nora Roberts is a master at this. Just when you think you see a cliché coming, her books go off in a completely new direction. Emma Darcy is another mould-breaker. In *The Wrong Mirror* (Darcy), she has a twin rush to the bedside of her dead twin's fiancé. Naturally, he mistakes her for her twin. The plot would have been hackneyed if left there, but the twin quickly disabuses him and the story goes its own original way.

Old ideas, new plots

Pondering one of the more common plot situations can provide you with an idea for a new story, provided you can come up with an original treatment of it. All of these situations have been used many times. How could you treat them differently?

- ♥ Man and woman stranded together on an island.
- ♥ Arranged or forced marriage.
- ♥ Pretending to be engaged or married.
- ♥ Woman or man seeking revenge on the other.
- ♥ Woman assumes another identity (e.g. twins).
- ♥ Unequal balance of power (e.g. a new boss).
- ♥ Tutor or nanny to hero's child.
- ♥ Secretary to an author.

♥ Hired to have his child (or she wants him to father hers).

♥ Secret baby—hero is unaware he's fathered a child.

♥ Royalty and commoner.

How can you turn these around? Perhaps the author is female and the secretary male. Better still, is he trying to prove she stole his ideas? The tutor or nanny to the hero's child might have been hired by his ex-wife (a close friend of hers) to prove he is an unfit parent. The possibilities are endless, provided you keep the focus on the developing romance.

Anne McAllister gives her own twist to the nanny theme in *The Playboy and the Nanny* when a sexy tycoon meets a gorgeous nanny and is thrown for a loop to learn his father has hired the lady to take care of him, not his four-year-old brother.

The desert island theme can be emotional as well as physical. In Anne Mather's *Leopard in the Snow*, the isolation came from the hero's withdrawal from society. A former racing driver, he was scarred in a serious accident. In *Sapphire Nights*, my hero and heroine had equally valid reasons for wanting to have an island to themselves. Here, I explored the old television comedy idea of putting a figurative white line down the middle of the property. The only common ground is the kitchen. This gives rise to some enjoyable scenes as they both find repeated excuses to go into the kitchen.

Social trends can inspire story ideas, another good reason to read widely and keep up with what is going on in society. The journal of the World Future Society reported a trend towards serial marriages, one after another, making me wonder how the children would cope.

This in turn inspired *Return to Faraway*, in which the heroine's marriage is threatened by the hero's teenage daughter from a previous marriage. The advent of the 'palimony suit' gave rise to the hero's retreat from the world after just such a legal battle in *Sapphire Nights*. What other trends or world events might inspire your plot?

As previously explained, it is better not to have your hero and heroine fighting all the time. Apart from the need to disagree over some real problem, they should have some concern in common which will eventually help to draw them together. In *Sapphire Nights*, my characters are both from the film world. She knows how it feels to be hounded by the media, so she helps the hero to elude it. In *Operation Monarch* both characters want to discover the truth about the hero's real parentage. Without some basis for commitment to develop, your love scenes can seem like sex for its own sake, rather than expressions of the deepening feelings between the characters.

The reason the hero and heroine can't get together—the conflict—must be strong enough to last the whole book through. If the conflict is resolved well before the end, you will be struggling to keep your characters apart. It's essential to have a good, strong problem which takes the whole book to solve.

Since it must be resolved by the end of the book, the conflict must be capable of resolution. This rules out the characters' disliking one another because of nationality, for example. If she hates Frenchmen *per se*, what is he— a Frenchman—to do about it? Far better to give her a distrust of married men. Even if she thinks he is married when they meet, and he doesn't tell her the truth for his own reasons, he can still come clean before the end of the book. If he's French, he will still be French on page 200.

There is no reason why your characters can't share a relationship that crosses cultural divisions, provided this isn't used as the conflict. Tanya Saari Starratt from Harlequin says writers are welcome to submit story ideas involving multicultural relationships provided this aspect isn't an issue in the story. 'This takes the focus from the hero and heroine's relationship and detracts from the story itself.'

In *Her Galahad*, Melissa James says her aim was to portray an Aboriginal hero without stereotypes, and saw category romance as 'the perfect platform':

> I took the best parts of their culture, threw out the bad and made [the hero] positive, strong, a tower of strength for his damaged heroine. Any time I fell into a trap [of stereotyping], I saw it and changed it. It must have worked because I'm getting terrific feedback, more on Jirrah than Tessa. I even got 'Jirrah is the perfect hero' from a reviewer.

Internal or external conflict?

Conflicts can be divided into two categories: internal and external. Internal conflicts are emotional in origin, usually resolved by the couple agreeing to accept each other's differences, gaining in maturity, or finding that they aren't as far apart emotionally as they first thought. Learning to trust again, restoring faith in one's self, and discovering inner strengths are all internal processes. In *Tasmanian Devil*, the heroine wants to prove her self-reliance. The hero's presence jeopardises her quest, but the main conflict is still internal.

External conflicts arise from sources outside the character. The stepdaughter problem in *Return to Faraway* is an example of external conflict. External conflicts include any barriers the characters face from outside themselves, such as previous romantic experiences, issues with children, or disagreements over property, family or careers. Often, there will be a combination of internal and external conflicts coming between the hero and heroine.

Whatever conflict you choose, the stakes must be high and the goal difficult to attain. It often pays to push the stakes beyond your first inclinations. In *That Midas Man*, the heroine has to interview the hero or lose a vital job promotion. At first glance, the job seemed enough motivation. But is a job offer sufficient to justify having her move heaven and earth to get the interview she needs? What if she needs the promotion for some other, more noble reason? I decided she needed the pay rise to have a fighting chance of regaining custody of her daughter from her wealthy ex-husband. With care and thought, you can usually think of ways to lift the stakes as high as possible, making for more compelling reading.

Outline the romance

Beware of having too much plot in a short romance. The story must always support and illuminate the romance, not overshadow it. To make sure you have the emphasis right, I suggest that you plot the romance as well as the story. How is this done? Simply make a list of the chapters, then summarise in a few words what happens to *the romance* in each chapter. If there is no development, the story may be getting in the way. Or you may not be using the story events to highlight the developing love story to best effect. The romance outline for *Tasmanian Devil* looked like this:

1   Evelyn discovers Dane on 'her' island. Her initial attraction is balanced by annoyance at his presence and at his refusal to leave.

2   She kisses him, trying to alarm him into leaving. It backfires when she finds herself enjoying it.

3   They dine together. She worries about the increasing strength of his attraction for her.

4   He massages her strained muscles, further turning her on, then invites her back to his cabin.

5   The intimacy leads to lovemaking, but she keeps her Cartier watch on, not having wholly committed herself to him.

6   Ex-boyfriend arrives and she uses him to make Dane jealous in a last-ditch bid to resist him.

7   She and Dane kiss passionately but he thinks it's more play-acting, of the kind she says she was doing with her ex-boyfriend.

8   Dane is cold towards her, thinking she's as scheming as his ex-wife.

9   She loves him but he wasn't honest with her. Their relationship seems to be at rock bottom with no hope.

10 She turns down job to stay with Dane whether he loves her or not. Of course he does. His coldness was also his defence against her.

You can see from this that none of the events in the story rates a mention unless it has a bearing on the developing romance. Outlining the romance separately from the story will show whether the love affair is moving too quickly, too slowly or just right. If a chapter goes by with no development in the romance, either good or bad, restructuring is needed.

Thinking through this aspect before you write your novel will help maintain a proper balance. If you have finished a manuscript, it may be worthwhile distilling out the romance elements to see whether your book is well balanced.

Some writing hints

Nora Roberts is good at keeping her hero and heroine together for as much of the book as possible. This is especially important in short romances, and explains why books where the characters work together or live under the same roof are so effective. Unless the couple have lots of valid reasons to get together, you will find yourself writing scene after scene where they bump into each other by chance, meet in restaurants and generally waste much time saying hello and goodbye.

I believe that the classic romance hero is frequently rich because it helps the author to keep the characters together. In the few books I've written in which the heroes actually work for a living, it becomes a challenge accounting for the time when they're supposed to be at work. Self-employed people are much more flexible and bosses don't have to account to others for their time, possibly the reason why so many lone wolves, corporate leaders and billionaires are cast as romantic heroes.

To enable you to keep the focus on the developing romance, the number of characters should be kept to a minimum. If you mention a maid and butler, for example, could they be compressed into one housekeeper? You may not need both a sister and an aunt for the heroine. The key scenes must always be given to the hero and heroine. They are the 'stars' of your production and should not be overshadowed by the other players. In too many manuscripts, the couple's parents are given scenes which belong to either the hero or the heroine. Even in longer novels, the lead characters should be responsible for working out their own destiny, free of outside interference. Other characters may set the wheels in motion, but should not do for the characters what they should do for themselves.

Think of yourself as a casting director, responsible for keeping the stars happy. Just as actors actually count the number of lines given to each character to make sure they aren't short-changed, you should ensure that your lead characters get the lion's share of the pages.

The relationship should also be even-sided, in keeping with modern mores. These days, the heroine wants the hero to enrich her life, not because she can't exist without him. She should be a willing participant in your love scenes, even if it's against her better judgement. If you've established her as a career woman, she probably shouldn't throw away her career to follow the hero, unless she has expressed doubts about her career all along. Occasionally, I've had the hero change *his* career plans so they can be together, or they've worked out a compromise. Her life shouldn't come to an end without him. The prospect may plunge her into gloom and it may not be the life she would choose, but she should be capable of going on.

Story structure

Start by hooking your reader, the how-to books tell you. But what is a hook and how do you write one? First, a narrative hook does not have to be action-packed or shocking, unless that is to be the tone of the rest of the book. A hook can be gentle and quiet, provided it grabs the reader's attention and doesn't let go. Some how-to books make a virtue of a brilliant first sentence. If you can write one, well and good. But a hook can also be several sentences or a whole paragraph, as long as the words skilfully lead the reader on until they're engrossed before they know it.

As any editor will tell you, too many romance novels start with a poetic description of a sunset, pages about the heroine getting up in the morning and preparing for work, or sitting in a train/plane/car, staring wistfully out at the passing scenery while thinking of how she came to be here and where she's going. In shorter books, you have very little time in which to capture the reader's attention. Every word must be used to maximum effect. Resist the temptation to tell the reader everything on the first page. Background information should be sprinkled sparingly throughout the book. It's much more important to introduce the reader to your heroine and bring in the background later, when the reader has had a chance to care about her.

To decide where to begin, choose a turning point in the heroine's life, a time at which things are changing for her, whether she likes it or not. If she doesn't like it, so much the better. She's going to be dragged into the change, kicking and screaming against her fate. The Romans called it *in medias res*, in the middle of things.

Maybe she's about to lose a job that she needs to support herself. Her company could be a takeover target and she doesn't like the new owners. Or a long-lost love may resurface in her life. The hero should be involved in the change in some way. He may head the takeover bid threatening her job. The long-lost love speaks for himself.

By starting in the middle of a change, then filling in the background a little at a time, you effectively hook your reader. Here are some narrative hooks which defy you not to keep reading.

From *Royal Spy*:

Gage Weston could think of worse ways to spend an afternoon than watching a princess get undressed. Sights like that were rare, even in his profession, but made putting his life on the line to spy for his country even more worthwhile.

From *The Tall, Dark Stranger*:

The first prediction came true on Monday night.

From *Man Without a Past*:

If they were going to murder her, Gaelle Maxwell wished they would hurry up and get it over with.

From *The Wrong Mirror* by Emma Darcy:

Kirsty was dying. Karen knew it even as she struggled into consciousness. Shock jerked her upright in bed. It was not a nightmare. She didn't know how she could be so sure, yet she was.

From *Another Time* by Susan Napier:

It was her. Alexander Knight stared at the photograph, the letter which had accompanied it crumpling in the involuntary fist of his left hand. Forgotten was the filthy Manhattan weather he had been fluently cursing when he had stormed into his ground-floor apartment, forgotten was the frustration he had just endured at the hands of an ill-informed television host, forgotten was the formal dinner he was already running late for, and the beautiful woman whom he had arranged to escort.

It was her.

All of these narrative hooks have one thing in common— they plunge the reader right into the middle of whatever is going on. In *The Wrong Mirror* (Darcy), we gradually learn that Kirsty is Karen's mirror-image twin and that they share an almost psychic bond. We know nothing else about them but it's impossible not to be caught up in Karen's frantic middle-of-the-night attempt to find out what has happened to her twin. Everything else can—and does—wait until we're enmeshed in the story.

Openings which start with a statement can startle the reader, as in *Man Without a Past*. They can arouse curiosity, as in *Royal Spy* and Susan Napier's prologue to *Another Time*. Most statement openings include some element which is out of the ordinary. If they are seemingly ordinary, they contain a suggestion that things won't be for long. The opening words of *Tasmanian Devil* are ordinary enough:

> As the green-clad mount of Frere Island appeared as a speck on the horizon, Evelyn Consett suppressed a shiver. It looked primitive and cold.

There's a wealth of suggestion in words like 'suppressed a shiver', 'primitive' and 'cold'. If it's so unappealing, why is she going there? Does she have a choice? What fate awaits her there?

If you choose to start with a description, make sure it is short and filled with a sense of more to come, or of peace soon to be shattered in some way.

Dialogue is another way to hook the reader. *Heartbreak Plains* opens with the words, 'Can't we go inside, just for a minute?' The question is not idle chatter. If the heroine's flatmate hadn't wanted to go into that particular shop, the heroine wouldn't be left alone outside, to be kidnapped in her flatmate's stead. The question is the catalyst which sets in motion all the events which follow.

By writing in the viewpoint of a key character from the very first words, as in the example from *Royal Spy,* you draw the reader straight into your fictional world. The opening paragraph of *Another Time* is written in the viewpoint of the hero, Alexander Knight. In a few lines, and in viewpoint, we learn that he is holding the photograph of a woman who is important to him. His reaction suggests that he has been looking for her for a long time.

We also learn, in viewpoint, that he is someone famous because he has been on television, that he has an apartment in New York, and that he has no shortage of beautiful escorts, otherwise he wouldn't treat them so cavalierly ('he was already running late'). He has a quick temper because he has been 'fluently cursing' the weather (fluently suggests he has lots of practice at it), and he doesn't suffer fools gladly, from the reference to an 'ill-informed television host'. What a lot we learn about Mr Knight in a short time. In fact, we learn everything we need to know at this point—and therein lies the key. There is no need to tell the reader everything about a character, only the facts they need to know at the start of the story.

To better grasp this necessity, imagine that your book is last night's television program. You have only a few minutes to tell your friend what went on. How much would you tell them about the lead character? Would you say something like, 'There was this journalist, just back from ten years in the Congo. The film started with him locating a woman he'd been searching for for years and it turned out she was engaged to his brother.' By summarising the opening of your own book in a similar way, you are more likely to zero in on the vital points which must be made so the reader knows what's going on. Any other details can be left until later in the story.

The reader must feel like a participant in the story, rather than reading about it second-hand. By hinting at more secrets to be revealed, you keep them turning the pages. This hinting is called 'foreshadowing'. You also raise questions in the reader's mind, as I did with the opening of *Tasmanian Devil*. Then you answer only enough of the questions to put the reader 'in the picture'. Tease them by withholding the rest of the answers so they are forced to read on to find out more. As soon as one question is answered, raise another. This is the 'domino effect' described by Anne Gisonny.

To see how it's done, compare the opening pages of books by your favourite authors. Note how information is infused gradually through dialogue and action rather than long, expository passages. When you write your own opening, be prepared to do several drafts until you get it just right. Then ask yourself which questions you have raised in the reader's mind that they must read on to answer. If they already know everything that's going on and it's obvious where the story is leading, they have no reason to keep reading. Provide one and you've got your opening hook.

What happens next?

Having hooked the reader, you must keep them entertained for 200 pages or so, until your hero and heroine declare their love on the last page.

Middle-page spread is a disease suffered by many new writers. They simply have no idea how to fill those middle chapters. The centre of the book becomes a holding action while the author tries desperately to think of new ways to keep the couple apart.

My first romance novels were full of picnics, balls, car rides and similar diversions to keep the lovers occupied. Now, before I start writing, I make sure that I have enough plot to keep the book moving under its own steam. Emma Darcy says:

> As a beginning writer, my own experience was that I could set up a great situation, but developing it into a full-length story was where the problems really started. I used to get my sister—now Miranda Lee—to read my work when I'd finished it. Too many times, she'd say, 'You had me for the first four chapters. Then the story seemed to meander, going around in boring circles until you decided to finish it.' I finally got the message that I had to seed more conflict which would grow and emerge in the middle to carry the story through to the end.

The secret is *cause and effect*. Something happens, therefore something else must happen, which leads to another event, and so on. The domino effect. The plot chart at the end of this chapter consists of hills and valleys. Each hill is higher and each valley deeper than the one before, until the characters hit 'rock bottom' and we think they are never going to resolve their problems and get together. Then the heroine pulls one last rabbit out of the hat and reaches her goal, free to love the man who has haunted her dreams since they met.

The heroine starts the book with a problem. In trying to solve it, she fails and makes matters worse. The next solution she tries is met with another failure, this time worse than the one before. In *Tasmanian Devil*, the heroine has a goal—a career and independence from her rich father. She reaches her first obstacle when she finds the hero sharing her island. Her solution—attempting to buy him off—not only fails, it makes him even more determined to stay.

She accepts this on the condition that he doesn't help her in any way. This solution leads directly to her next barrier—she won't let him fix her roof so it falls in, making her plight worse than before.

This problem is overcome and things look promising, but then she reaches the biggest barrier—it seems the hero is her father's henchman. This brings her to the rock bottom of despair, often called 'the black moment'. Her turning point is finding, inside herself, the determination to finish her month on the island. This character change sows the seeds of her eventual triumph. But there's a last twist and a final obstacle. She turns down the job she's worked so hard to attain, finding that she wants the hero more, but he has vanished. Using all her wiles, she locates him. He admits that he loves her—his coldness was a defence against her—and they are free to plan their future together.

Each time the heroine reaches a barrier, she must overcome it, only to find a more daunting one in her way. Then she must find her own solution, usually through a character change or flash of insight, to win through.

When planning these scenes, I find it useful to focus on the *work* each piece of writing has to do. If my heroine must discover that her lover is in her father's employ, I can choose how she finds out. The hero could tell her himself. But there would be no conflict in that. She could overhear it, read about it in an old magazine while cleaning the budgie cage—no drama there, either. Or someone could tell her with the intention of hurting her or coming between her and her goal. I chose this last option for its drama and interest. By concentrating on what you need to achieve with a particular scene, you will be much more aware of your writing options.

Think of the barriers as hurdles your heroine must jump in order to reach her heart's desire. There should not be more than two or three in a short romance or the story will feel repetitious and the reader will be frustrated by the lack of progress. Remember, two steps forward and one step back. She may not be making much progress, but there is always a little. Each barrier she overcomes brings her a little closer to her goal.

The importance of pace

According to Harlequin Mills & Boon, the pace of your novel should be like the ebb and flow of the tide. Some scenes ripple, others crash like the surf. There are moments of conflict and moments of rapport when the characters have time to get to know and eventually love each other. Using the hills-and-valleys approach to plotting, you can see how to fit in these moments of rapport—when all seems to be going well—before the next valley strikes. The growing closeness will make the next barrier all the more dramatic. She cares more about him, therefore she has more to lose.

The plot chart in this chapter shows how you can build in these hills and valleys to add pace and excitement to your novel. The plot should never chug along smoothly, all on the same plane, with occasional flutters and worries but no major concerns or moments of high emotion. Have you ever seen anyone sleep on a roller-coaster? Neither will they nod off through your book if you plot in the highs and lows, making the highs higher and the lows lower with each new development.

The highs and lows can be emotional as well as physical, as you've seen in the examples given. If you're writing an intrigue or suspense novel, the highs and lows may well involve action and adventure and actual danger, but in sub-genres such as chick lit, the threat may be to the heroine's peace of mind or to her best-laid plans. Whatever action she chooses to take to overcome her barriers, make sure it is solidly motivated. Ordinary people do not walk into a hail of bullets unless a child is in danger or there is some other equally strong motivation forcing their hand.

You can keep interest high in your books by providing a 'cliffhanger' at the end of each chapter. Sometimes, I use a surprise: the heroine finds out that the hero is working with her father. Or a question: 'What on earth was she going to do now?' Or a line of dialogue: 'He ignored her halting attempt to apologise, continuing his relentless progress until her back met cold, unyielding marble. "What was that about submissive?"'

Check to see how your favourite authors handle chapter endings. Chances are that they will use some of the devices above, or something similar, so it's almost impossible not to read on. Here are a few more examples.

From *The Tiger's Lair* by Helen Bianchin:

'It's quite simple,' he drawled. 'I want you to live with me as my wife.'

From *Loving* by Penny Jordan:

> She hadn't meant to encourage the little girl to love her, but how much damage had she inadvertently done?

From my book *Interrupted Lullaby*:

> The unkind things Zeke had written in his column would pale into insignificance beside his reaction when he knew she had kept from him the birth of his own child.

From *Bride of Diamonds* by Emma Darcy:

> 'Let's go straight to the heart of the matter, Miss Hammond. Only it's not Miss Hammond, is it? It's Miss McKenzie. The daughter of Andrew McKenzie.'

And this gem from *Long Time Coming* by Sandra Brown:

> Crooking a finger beneath her chin, he tilted her head up. 'Is he my son?'
> Marnie looked directly into his eyes and answered, 'Yes.'

More often than not, a chapter will end on a question, if not literally, then by planting one in the reader's mind. You should always write up to a chapter ending, not wind down. In a sense, they are like mini-endings in themselves, resolving one problem only to raise another, even bigger one.

Weaving a thread of mystery through your love story also keeps interest high, especially if the mystery concerns the hero. Is he all that he seems? In *Tasmanian Devil*, it looks as if the hero is working for the heroine's father, to prevent her reaching her goal. All the 'facts' seem to point to it and Dane himself doesn't deny it. We later discover this is his way of keeping some distance between them. He is also falling in love and resisting it. It is up to Evelyn to decide whether the truth is more important than her growing love for Dane. For the reader, the interest lies in how she resolves her dilemma.

The turning point which brings the heroine's goal within reach should be attained by her own efforts or by the character change which makes it possible. Readers have little patience with characters who wake up to find 'it was all a dream'. If Dane hadn't been working with Evelyn's father, it would be a tiresome misunderstanding. Nor should a third party intervene at the last moment and solve everyone's problems. The third party may provide the ammunition—just as the fairy godmother provided Cinderella with her own gown and coach—but the characters themselves must work out their own problems if the book is to reach a truly satisfying conclusion.

Happy endings

Above all else, the ending must *satisfy* the reader. Whether you leave them on a high of happiness and excitement, in a dreamy, hand-holding mood, aroused because the hero and heroine have just made passionate love, or smiling at the foibles of the chick lit world, the ending must feel right. This quality of 'feeling right' will require practice to develop. I sometimes rewrite the last few sentences of a book a dozen times before it has a perfect ring to it. It must sound as if there is nothing more to be said, no more questions to be answered, at least at this stage of the characters' lives. They have reached their goals and found each other. What more could you want?

If it's true that the beginning sells the writer's current book, then the ending sells your next book. It's the scene which will linger longest in the reader's mind, so it should be truly memorable, written with all the romance and poetry in your soul.

Good endings don't happen by themselves. They must be thought through to the last detail, resolving all the loose threads of your plot, explaining away all the misunderstandings, and finally reaffirming your theme that love conquers all.

Ideally, the main characters' goals should be achieved just a short time before they resolve their problems with each other. Otherwise their love may appear to be conditional. If you let me keep my wilderness intact, I will love you. If you gain custody of my child for me, I will love you. In *That Midas Man*, my heroine's goal is to regain custody of her child from her wealthy ex-husband. In the course of achieving this goal, she falls deeply in love with the hero. At the end of the book, he proposes marriage to her and there is the suggestion that he will help her regain her child. Why didn't I include the child in a nice, tidy closing package? I didn't want it to appear as if the heroine was marrying him for the wrong reasons. She loves him whether or not he is able to get her child back. I deliberately left the child question unresolved so that her love comes with no strings attached.

If the romance is the core of the story, the resolution of the romance should end the story. No matter what other threads you weave through your plot, they should not overshadow the romance and they should be resolved before the romance is resolved. Solving a business dilemma or some other problem should be incidental to the couple working out their real problem—their future together.

Almost invariably, your hero and heroine should be alone in the closing scene. This is their big moment. Minor characters can be accounted for in their dialogue, or can pop in and then out of the scene with some clue as to where they are going. You should leave enough pages to allow you to explore the happy ending fully. It should never be rushed. The reader has stayed with your characters through many pages of struggle and torment while the two were kept apart by ever-increasing obstacles. They are entitled to a long, leisurely finale as the characters come closer and closer together, stripping away each last, lingering doubt until none remains.

To get full value out of your ending, you must milk it for every nuance of emotion. Allow your heroine to tease the hero a little, perhaps suggesting that some barrier believed overcome is still there. When he realises she is teasing him, he will take his revenge in the sweetest, most loving way. He may tease her as well. They could review together the dark moments in their relationship when they thought things would never work out. She may confess the fears she harboured during those times, enabling him to reassure her that she need never doubt him again.

I like my endings to recap some of the themes of the book, as in this closing scene from *Interrupted Lullaby*:

> When she could breathe again, she said, "I thought you didn't believe in always."
>
> "You made me believe. For richer and poorer, good and bad, until death do us part." He lifted his head. "Tell me it's what you want, too?"

She rested her head against him. "It's what I've always dreamed of with you."

He tilted her chin up. "Just goes to show you, dreams can come true."

"Ours have, all of them."

"Not quite. Brendan is still an only child."

But not for long, she thought as Zeke's arms came around her and his mouth found hers. Not for long.

While not all romance novels have to end with a marriage proposal nowadays, the final moments should hold the promise that whatever comes next for your hero and heroine will be worthwhile. In a chick lit novel, the heroine has grown and learned from the experiences you've given her, and her life is now moving into a new phase filled with fresh promise. This is a fantasy, and the readers want to believe your characters will eventually find happiness.

Plot checklist

♥ Do your hero and heroine meet as close to page one as possible? Does the reader share the characters' immediate attraction to one another, shown through their viewpoints and senses?

♥ Is the conflict between them original, or given a fresh twist?

♥ Do you show the conflict through their actions and dialogue?

♥ Do you show how they resolve the conflict through their own efforts, leaving them free to love?

♥ Is there a balance of fast-paced scenes and quiet moments—hills and valleys—in your plot?

♥ Is there a balance between narrative passages and dialogue?

♥ Will you need to rewrite long paragraphs of narrative to make shorter ones, or can they be rewritten in dialogue?

♥ Have you started the book with a 'hook' and ended each chapter on a cliffhanger or question so we'll want to read on?

♥ Does the plot follow the domino effect of each action leading to the next, which leads to something else, and so on?

♥ Is the focus kept on the developing romance throughout, with your hero and heroine thrown together as much as possible?

♥ Have you 'charted' the romance to make sure it develops steadily and convincingly from first kiss to satisfactory ending?

♥ At the conclusion, have you tied up all the loose ends, cleared up any misunderstandings and followed through any foreshadowed plot points?

♥ Is the ending romantic and worth waiting for? Is it long enough and sensuous enough to reward the reader with a truly satisfying conclusion, leaving them uplifted by the experience?

Plot chart

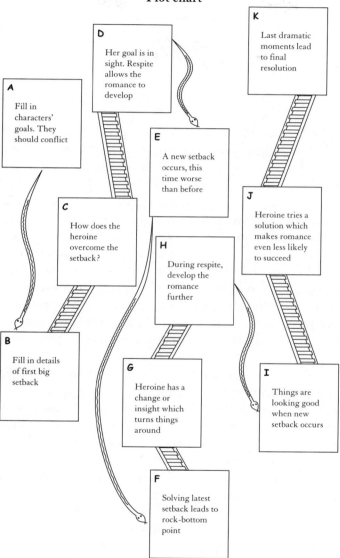

K Last dramatic moments lead to final resolution

D Her goal is in sight. Respite allows the romance to develop

A Fill in characters' goals. They should conflict

E A new setback occurs, this time worse than before

J Heroine tries a solution which makes romance even less likely to succeed

C How does the heroine overcome the setback?

H During respite, develop the romance further

B Fill in details of first big setback

G Heroine has a change or insight which turns things around

I Things are looking good when new setback occurs

F Solving latest setback leads to rock-bottom point

7
Setting

For many years, one of the appeals of romance novels was their ability to transport readers to some exotic place or take them behind the scenes of an intriguing profession, far away from everyday concerns. In line with the faster tempo of modern life, this appeal is less important. As more people travel routinely or have interesting professions themselves, the need for this form of escapism is lessening.

Traditional romances have also become shorter in word count and the pace faster than in previous years, leaving you less room to describe settings in great detail. Also, everyday settings and characters have become more acceptable in books such as chick lit, where readers prefer the backgrounds and situations to reflect their own experiences.

These changes don't mean that your choice of background is unimportant. Only that your descriptions need to be shorter and the details more carefully blended with the story. As one editor observed, 'The background is the background.' By this, he meant it should stay in the background and not overwhelm the book. You are writing a romance which happens to be set on a cruise ship, not a story about a cruise on which two people meet.

Any detail you mention should enhance the story, so choose settings which add tension, glamour, mystery or excitement. This applies to individual scenes as well as to the book as a whole. A scene in which the hero and heroine are arguing about work could well take place in the heroine's office. However, if tradesmen are working there and the scene is moved to her home, the scene becomes fraught with tension, especially if his presence makes her all too aware of the bedroom she can glimpse through a half-open door.

Each publisher has different requirements regarding backgrounds. They are usually spelled out in the writers' guidelines. Some US publishers want only American settings or require at least part of the story to be set in the United States. Others welcome international settings. Be guided by the tip sheet and don't submit material that contravenes the basic requirements.

If you know your characters well, the background will often choose itself. Writing about a farmer with a passion for conservation, I chose the Riverina district of New South Wales as my setting because the farmers there face serious environmental challenges such as erosion and salinity of the soil. It was a 'natural' choice. Another story, *Heartbreak Plains*, demanded total isolation, so I chose the Nullarbor Plain, and gained a title into the bargain (Heart-break Plains was a nickname given to the Nullarbor in colonial times because of its hostility to settlers).

This doesn't mean that every book needs an unusual setting. With readers in every country of the world, every-where is exotic to someone. A reader in India wrote to Harlequin asking for more Scottish settings. Australians find the outback unremarkable, but American readers can't get enough of it. Your familiar locale is bound to be new and different to someone.

Readers still enjoy gaining insights into unusual places or professions, provided the book doesn't become a

travelogue with huge chunks of information straight out
of the guide books. There are many ways to describe your
backdrop other than in unrelieved narrative. One is to
allow the details to come through while your characters
are in action. The reader learns about a place almost
without being aware of it. In this scene from *Operation
Monarch*, Garth and Serena are on an undercover mission
to rescue a couple from their kidnappers.

The ranger's cabin was on the sheltered side of the cay. She
had landed on the windy south side, where the trees were
stunted and distorted into fantastic shapes by the prevailing
winds. Her heart jerked as a diamond-shaped ray lifted
from the rocky bottom, its long tail grazing her leg.

She made an effort to steady her breathing. Garth was
doing his part, taking the boat around the island to where
a rickety jetty jutted into the sea, making his lone-
fisherman act look good. Soon she could see him only in
silhouette against the blood orange of the setting sun as
he let the boat drift close to the jetty. Anyone watching was
bound to get antsy about seeing him there, but that was the
idea.

She slogged through the water feeling the level reef
rocks gradually give way to sloping sandy beach. Sea
cucumbers lay like thick, dark sausages on the bottom. She
dodged them and tried not to twist an ankle in the craters
in the sand among dugong grass that provided home for the
crabs that were just starting their nocturnal activities.

More worrying were the stone fish camouflaging
themselves by lying completely flat on the sand or in the
rubble on the reef flat. There was no way to beware of
them, and their poisonous spines could spear through
shoes. They did not use their spines to attack, but waited to

snap up small fish as they swam past the deceptive 'stone'. Antivenom was available on the mainland but the painful effects of an encounter were well enough known to make her wary.

She released a breath as she emerged onto dry land, having avoided the ocean's numerous traps. How could Garth take such risks and call it fun? She glanced to where she could see his silhouette as he cast his line close to shore. He would keep up his act until she'd had time to get the Pascales out of the cabin and down to the rendezvous point, she knew.

I could have described the ocean creatures and scenery in pretty, poetic narrative, but, by making them a scary backdrop for Serena's landing on the island, they become much more effective as a tool to heighten her sense of danger. As far as possible, descriptions should be written in viewpoint, as in this example. The need to describe what a character sees, hears, smells and feels automatically limits the details you include and helps you to judge how much to use.

Australian settings are still enormously popular among readers in other countries, so there's no need to set your story in America or the Greek islands unless you know these places well. It's also fine to use real locations, providing you describe them in flattering terms. Restaurants, places of business and specific streets may be better if invented, both to avoid legal problems and to give you more freedom to create them to your own requirements. I have invented islands, towns and even whole countries. My South Pacific island kingdom of Carramer, the setting for a number of Silhouette romances about the Carramer royal family, is my own invention, although it conforms to the flora, fauna and climate of similar islands in the same vicinity. It's a good idea to check maps of the area concerned to ensure that the place you thought you invented doesn't already exist.

Professions

As with the setting, the careers you choose for your characters should enhance the flavour of the book. The days when all heroines were secretaries, nannies or pampered heiresses and all heroes were powerful father figures are mercifully gone. And you would need very good reasons to place a modern-day heroine under the guardianship of a man. While the medical world is an increasingly popular backdrop for romance novels, today both hero and heroine are likely to be doctors, or enjoy equal professional standing in some other aspect of medicine.

So what has replaced the timeworn occupations of earlier romance novels? Almost any career you can think of. There are romances about Antarctic scientists, helicopter pilots, zookeepers, deep-sea divers and psychic detectives. A whole sub-genre has developed around characters serving in the military in various countries. Provided the career background isn't allowed to overshadow the developing romance, readers enjoy a glimpse into a different world.

Some professions seem to be more popular with readers than others. Actors seldom rate highly, perhaps because of the much-married Hollywood image. Plain-clothes detectives may also be difficult to cast as heroines, because of a preconception, accurate or not, that there is little room in their lives for romance. After women began to serve in the space program, there was a rash of female astronauts. However, the job was simply too far removed from the reader's experience to make for easy identification. This is not to say that you should not write about these, or any other, professions. As Silhouette Executive Editor, Leslie Wainger, puts it, 'It's all in the execution.'

A perception is that a certain toughness is required for some jobs, leaving little room for love and romance. Rightly or wrongly, it's hard to imagine a romance in which the heroine is a prison guard, for instance. We would be too aware of the realities of her job to fantasise about it.

Again, bear in mind that the characters will need to be together for much of the book, so choose professions where this is at least possible. A doctor on night shift and a busy executive would have a hard time seeing enough of each other to fall in love!

I enjoy the idea of readers being inspired to enter a particular profession after reading one of my books, so I try to make my portrayals as accurate as possible. And in my private crusade against female stereotyping, I make minor characters—doctors, lawyers and the like—female. In one book, my heroine's closest friend is an electrician running her own company.

Getting the facts right

Whatever setting or career background you choose, make sure you do your homework. It's a myth that romance novels are 'dashed off' with little work or forethought. Your research may include scouring hundreds of Internet sites, reading dozens of books, interviewing people in particular jobs and, wherever possible, visiting the settings of your books.

Even if I know a place well, I still contact the local tourist advisory centre for current information, in case anything has changed since my visit. Thanks to the Internet, almost any detail can now be confirmed without leaving your desk.

When setting a book in a real place, never take anything for granted. Just because a map of a country town shows a railway station, don't have your character arriving by train without ensuring that the station still functions. Some have been closed for years. Check and double-check place names and titles, especially foreign words. A romance writer was taken to task for leaving the final 's' off Champs-Elysées. Investing in a copy of *The Oxford Dictionary for Writers and Editors* will save you making mistakes like this one.

Finally, remember to glamorise your setting. Heat, dust and flies may be accurate, but are they romantic? Use the written equivalent of the filmic 'soft focus' and show us a place where love can bloom.

Art brief

An art brief guides the cover artist and writer of the cover notes, known as 'the blurb'. Creating an art brief for your own book is useful practice and helps you to keep track of key details.

Book title:
Author:
Setting:
Season/month:
Duration of story:
Main conflict:

Heroine's name:
Age:
Occupation:
Character type:
Height/body type:
Hair colour and style:
Eye colour:

Hero's name:
Age:
Occupation:
Character type:
Height/body type:
Hair colour and style:
Eye colour:

Suitable cover scene (including clothes, jewellery, make-up and props)

8

Query and outline

lthough the words are often interchanged, I prefer to think of an outline as a chapter-by-chapter breakdown of a book, and a synopsis as a summary of the highlights. An outline is the equivalent of a painter's preliminary sketches, guiding the writer through the manuscript. The synopsis is more often a selling tool, polished as carefully as the finished manuscript and submitted to an editor as part of a proposal.

Publishers seldom go to contract on the basis of a proposal, although it does happen, but at least it will save you wasting months of hard work to find out that the book is unsuitable for a particular imprint. If the editor likes the synopsis, you'll receive at least some encouragement and possibly some specific pointers towards eventual acceptance.

When writing the synopsis, think of yourself as writing the copy for the jacket of a book. Imagine you're a reader browsing in a bookstore. What would make you want to buy this book? The main difference between jacket copy and the synopsis is the need to tie up all the loose ends. No editor wants to be told to 'read the book to find out what happens next'. The editor wants to see proof of your writing style and ability to bring the book to a successful conclusion.

For a short contemporary romance, the outline should be no longer than two or three pages. It should explain:

- ♥   who the hero and heroine are
- ♥   how they come together (with a suggestion of the setting)
- ♥   the nature of the conflict between them
- ♥   how they resolve the conflict through their own efforts
- ♥   brief details of any subplots
- ♥   the satisfactory/happy ending.

Your synopsis should sketch in enough of the characters' backgrounds to explain their actions (their motivation). Use sparing amounts of dialogue, if you wish, to bring the characters to life. Doing this in the space of a synopsis is a real challenge but it is far more important than wasting words on poetic physical descriptions and scenery. Refer to your character charts and include the most telling details of their personalities in your synopsis.

In a couple of pages, you won't have room to describe every event in your novel. Go back to the plot chart. The hills and valleys you've filled in are probably the scenes you should include, as these are the ones which drive the story forward.

Try to open your synopsis with a hook, as you would the manuscript. This serves the same purpose of grabbing the editor's attention and making them want to read on. Minor characters should be sketched in briefly, in relation to the hero and heroine. Sometimes, you won't even want to name them, describing them as 'Jenny's brother' or 'the postman'.

A synopsis is not set in concrete. Provided the book you submit is essentially the same as the one in the synopsis, editors accept that characters grow and change during the writing and that events take different turns.

How to present your synopsis

A synopsis is traditionally written in third person, present tense: Jack announces he's leaving; Jenny begs him to stay. This gives your synopsis a sense of excitement and immediacy, and saves words.

The format is the same as for a manuscript page. Allow wide (at least 2 cm) margins all around, with the book title, author's name and page number at the top of each sheet, and a title page showing the book title, your name and contact details, pen-name if used, and estimated number of words in the finished manuscript.

Some editors say they prefer single-spaced synopses, others like to see double spacing, so there's no 'correct' method. I use single spacing for the simple reason that synopses are not edited (the reason for double spacing manuscript pages is to allow for editorial comments and annotations).

As for every piece of work you submit, use good quality paper of A4 size and clear printing on one side of the paper only. Make sure there are no spelling or typographical errors. Beware of relying too heavily on a computer spellchecker which makes no distinction between word meanings such as 'their' and 'they're'. It's worth the extra time and care to present a polished, professional image.

The majority of publishers, other than those operating primarily online, prefer not to receive submissions from new writers via email or on disk, although they may accept both from writers with whom they have an established working relationship. Most also ask you not to send multiple submissions—that is, manuscripts that have been submitted to more than one publisher for consideration at any one time.

The proposal

A proposal, also known as a partial, consists of a covering letter, a synopsis and sample chapters (usually about 50 pages of the finished book). Individual publishers' requirements are specified in their writers' guidelines. Some Harlequin Mills & Boon lines, for example, ask to see three sample chapters; others prefer you to submit the finished manuscript. Many publishers prefer to see only a query or synopsis first, and will tell you if they wish to see more. Three sample chapters always means the first three chapters in order, not three chosen at random. Print the chapters using double spacing, even if the synopsis and query letter are single spaced. Do not leave extra spacing between paragraphs. Indicate paragraph starts by indenting.

The query letter

More and more, publishers are asking to see a query letter before inviting you to submit a partial. There are two schools of thought as to what makes the perfect query letter. Some writers prefer a businesslike tone, others use the letter to showcase their writing talents. I prefer a mixture of both.

Try to keep your letter to a single page, editing it until you've said everything you need to say. This not only shows your professionalism but will be appreciated by an overworked editor. Print the letter on plain white bond paper. Butterflies or fancy stationery don't help your professional image. A business-type letterhead is fine if you have it.

Important elements to include in your letter are:

♥ A brief summary of your book, why it's special, what is new, different or distinctive about it, and why you think it suits this publisher. If appropriate, you might mention some of the 'hooks' contained in your story, such as 'secret baby', 'royalty' or 'twins separated at birth'. These are discussed more fully in Chapter 9, 'A Pitch in Time'. Also state if you have completed the manuscript.

♥ Your writing credentials. If you are published, briefly summarise your writing credits. If you're unpublished, mention writing courses you've done and any professional writing groups you belong to. Don't say this is your first novel or that you're only a beginner. Be positive.

♥ Your credentials can include prizes in romance-related competitions, short stories you've had published—even if they're in small-press magazines—and newsletter-writing for organisations, provided it is relevant.

♥ Your interest in the romance genre, perhaps as an avid reader with a keen interest in this particular line. This shows awareness of the publisher's needs and familiarity with their work.

♥ Any professional credentials which qualify you to write this book. If you're an accountant and the book is about a tax agent going undercover at the hero's corporation, your background would stand you in good stead.

Make sure your query and proposal are addressed to the current editor of the line or imprint. There is nothing more annoying to an editor than receiving submissions meant for their predecessor, especially if they left three years ago. It's a simple matter to contact the publisher on the day you send your submission, and ask for confirmation of the spelling and title of the person to whom you're sending your work.

If return postage is requested and you are submitting a partial or full manuscript to London or North America, you may find it more economical to include enough coupons to cover correspondence only, and retain a copy of the manuscript in your files. Mention this in your letter to show that you are aware of the professional courtesies.

A response to a query may take six to eight weeks. A response to a proposal will take longer, and to a completed manuscript up to several months. For peace of mind, it's acceptable to include a self-addressed postcard with sufficient return postage for the receiving person to let you know your material is safely in their hands.

Publishers receive thousands of queries, partials and manuscripts a year, so considering them takes time. Harlequin Mills & Boon reads everything submitted and will help and encourage any author whom it believes has the potential to fulfil its publishing needs. This means that if you receive any sort of specific comment, you can be quite heartened. Unfortunately, rejections seem to come back more quickly than good news—or maybe it only seems that way!

Sample synopsis

This is an example of the type of plot and character details to include in a synopsis that is intended to interest a publisher in a short romance novel.

Outline for The Baby Secret by Valerie Parv:

Who is Jake McVey? For 24 years she believed she was the child of Texan ranchers. On their deaths, she discovers she was born in Australia and adopted by the McVeys. She also discovers she has a twin sister. Deciding to search for her family, she leaves the ranch in the care of her brother and signs on as a trainee with the International Agricultural Exchange Association, specifying a farming interest which will take her to the Gundagai region of New South Wales, where she was born. To avoid recognition, she uses her nickname, Jake, on the forms.

She is met at the airport by Nash Campbell, owner of her host property, Kookaburrah. Expecting a man, Nash is taken aback by Jake, and also feels there is something familiar about her. Finally, he guesses who she is and refuses to take her to Kookaburrah. She forces him to by threatening to reveal who she is. His adopted sister, Chris, is her twin but doesn't know she's adopted, so he takes Jake's threat seriously. Nash's mother, an invalid, has made him promise not to tell Chris about her background. He regrets the promise now, made in his teens, as he thinks she has a right to know, but he cannot put his mother's health at risk.

He warns her he intends to pose as her admirer in order to keep a close eye on her. His sister, a charter pilot, is away when they reach Kookaburrah. His mother is also away so there is no chance Jake's identity will be discovered. When she finally meets Chris, it is almost too much for Jake, knowing she can't reveal their relationship. They become instant friends, however. When Chris accidentally finds out that they share the same birthday, she plans a joint party. Nash is against it but Chris prevails. During the party, Jake is strongly attracted to Nash but blames her attraction on his vow 'to keep an eye on her'. He is impressed when she has an opportunity to tell Chris who she is but keeps her word.

Working with him on the property, Jake earns Nash's reluctant respect. She helps him to catch thieves who have been stealing stock. Nash is injured and Jake takes over his office work as well as her own outdoor tasks. Catching Jake asleep at the desk, he reads her the riot act, only hearing later from Chris how hard she has been working. To make amends he takes her to a cattle auction in town, followed by a romantic dinner. They stay in town overnight and she discovers she has fallen in love with him.

Returning to the property, they discover that Nash's mother is coming home unexpectedly. Jake knows she must leave but is bitter when Nash makes no move to stop her, even lending her a vehicle.

In town, she overhears men planning to get even with Nash for catching their friends, the rustlers. She tries to contact him without success. She decides that, whatever the cost, she must go back and warn him of the trap. Nash turns up in time to save her from the rustlers who have cornered her. She's exhausted so he takes her back to the homestead and puts her in his own bed. His mother is ill with a virus so is unlikely to meet Jake. Nash watches over her and during the night, she awakens. The pull is too strong and they make love.

Next morning, Jake decides to leave but is intercepted by Nash. He tells her they have to work this out. She assumes he means the traineeship, which she offers to give up. He says it isn't that, he wants her to stay. But how can she when she cannot acknowledge Chris as her sister?

There is a cry behind them. Chris has heard everything. She takes off in her old Tiger Moth, a plane she keeps for enjoyment, and flies recklessly over the property. Nash and Jake plead with her by radio and finally she lands but a tyre blows out and it is touch and go whether she'll make it back safely. The tension destroys the final barriers between Nash and Jake. Chris survives the rough landing and accepts the situation. The stunt flying was her way of coping with the discovery of her adoption.

Chris is delighted to have Jake as a sister, always having sensed there was a special bond between them. Nash tells her he intends to marry Jake, if she'll have him. Jake accepts his proposal joyfully. In the outback, she has found her past and a more wonderful future than she ever dreamed was possible.

Sample query letter

Professional opening.

Date   Your name
Publisher's name   and address
and address

Dear (editor's name)

I am a keen reader of your Love Heart line and I feel that my book <u>The Baby Secret</u>, a romance involving twins separated at birth, may meet your needs.

Who is Jake McVey? For 24 years she believed she was the daughter of Texan ranchers. On their death, she finds she is Australian by birth and sets out to find her roots.

In Australia, her main obstacle is the formidable property owner, Nash Campbell, who does all he can to thwart her quest. His adopted sister is Jake's twin. Jake's presence threatens his family stability. However, her determination wins his respect and finally, his love. But by then, Jake's research has shown that she could be Nash's half-sister. She discovers that Nash's mother falsified her birth records in order to keep Jake's twin after she lost her own child to cot death. Jake and Nash are free to love in the land down under at long last.

For five years I have been a regular reader of the Love Heart series, and won the Woman's Realm romance competition in 2002. I have completed two professional-level writing courses and am a member of Romance Writers of Australia. My experience as an adoption counsellor inspired me to write <u>The Baby Secret</u>. As noted in your writers' guidelines, I am enclosing a two-page synopsis and three sample chapters for your consideration. The 65 000 word manuscript is completed and available upon request. I have included international reply coupons for correspondence only. The material may be recycled should it not meet your needs.

Thank you for taking the time to consider my proposal.

Yours faithfully,

Sheila B. Wright

Sheila B. Wright

Describes main characters, conflict and resolution.

Writing credentials and professional associations. Familiarity with their requirements.

9

A pitch in time

This chapter could have been headed 'How to sell your book in ten minutes' because that's all the time you're usually given to pitch your book idea to an agent or editor at a writer's conference.

The idea of pitching—or giving a verbal synopsis of your book to an editor or agent—started with scriptwriters in Hollywood. In the US Writers' Guild regulations are strict about how much work a scriptwriter can be asked to do before they must be paid. Asking a writer to pitch an idea was not considered a commission, so the pitch was born. These days it's quite usual for editors and agents to make themselves available to meet writers at conferences, either through individual or group appointments. This is one of the best chances you'll ever have to meet an editor or agent and get them excited about reading your book proposal, so it should not be wasted.

Preparation is the key to successful pitching. It starts with deciding which romance line best suits your work. Check with conference organisers to see if an editor for that line will be taking appointments with writers. If not, will an editor from the same publisher be willing to accept pitches for your chosen line as well as their own? This is not ideal, but still beats sending out your work without some advance preparation. And if the editor or agent asks to see more, you can write 'requested material' on the envelope when you send them your manuscript, bypassing the unsolicited slush pile.

It's a good idea to look up an agent or editor in a marketing guide such as *Romance Writers Report*, to find out what they're interested in buying. Writers' centres and organisations such as the Australian Society of Authors can provide lists of agents. You can also gain more information by consulting publishers' websites.

Be aware that editors usually prefer writers to have the completed manuscript ready for submission before pitching. Conference organisers sometimes ask that you only request an editor or agent appointment when you have completed the book. Tracey Farrell, executive editor for both Harlequin Historicals and HQN, Harlequin's mainstream romance imprint, suggests that writers consult publishers' guidelines before scheduling an appointment. She says she will accept queries from published authors, but requires completed manuscripts from newcomers. However, you should not bring the manuscript to the appointment. Nor should you bring gifts for the editor, however well meant. The only item you should expect to leave with them is a professional-looking business card.

Apply for your appointment as early as you possibly can as slots are limited and invariably fill quickly. If you can't get a one-on-one appointment, don't despair. Many editors prefer appointments with a group of writers anyway, and this can be less daunting if you are the nervous type. You can also learn a great deal from listening to other writers make their pitches.

The founder of Romance Writers of New Zealand, Jean Drew, suggests you think of your appointment as a business meeting, and adopt a businesslike approach.

Dressing professionally, introducing yourself with a hand-shake and a smile, and acting confident, even if it's the last thing you feel, will all help to break the ice. Editors I've spoken to about these appointments say they are often just as nervous as you are. They are also equally anxious to be the one to discover the next international bestselling author.

Keep it simple

Avon author, Michele Albert, also known as Michelle Jerott, says you should keep your pitch simple.

> Don't bog yourself down with unnecessary back story, secondary characters and subplots. All the editor wants to know is if you have a good grasp of your main characters, a balance of internal/external conflict, and the story's marketing angle ('hook'). Five to ten minutes is plenty of time, so speak slowly, maintain eye contact, and allow time for questions.

Michele says the pitch for her book *A Great Catch* would read like this:

> After years of working her way upward in the male-dominated maritime world of Great Lakes shipping, Tessa Jardine lands her dream job as First Mate on the passenger ship SS TALIESIN—a dream job until she meets her captain, Lucas Hall. Ten years ago Lucas broke her young heart when he walked away from her without a word of farewell, and she can't forgive him for that—or for his more recent part in a failed rescue attempt that cost her younger brother his life. Now Lucas, the ex-Coast Guard hero, is back to complicate her life. Working together day after day,

Lucas and Tessa discover the attraction between them is still hot and heavy—but can Tessa forgive Lucas, or ever learn to trust him again. And what will Lucas have to do to win back her love?

In creating this summary, Michele broke down the content of her book to situation (the dream job which involves working for her former love), character (Tessa and Lucas) and conflict, (the difficulty of working day to day with a man she doesn't trust, but still finds disturbingly attractive).

You could also add a sentence or two about the main crisis between your lead characters and how they resolve their differences.

Since your time is limited, it can help to include in your pitch some 'story hooks', a term for elements that define the theme of a category romance quickly and succinctly. Sure, these are clichés and you wouldn't want to pepper your writing with them, but they can be useful short cuts to get your ideas across. Think of them as a kind of romance industry shorthand.

Examples of 'story hooks' you might mention in your pitch, assuming your plot includes them, are: secret babies (suggesting a child the hero doesn't know he's fathered), single dads, amnesia, twins, cowboys, switched-at-birth, weddings and brides, marriage of convenience, royal, doctor, cop, small-town setting, ranch, military, Cinderella, Beauty and the Beast. All these elements are identified with romance novels, and are still perennially popular with readers. Try to show how your interpretation of the chosen hook is unique.

These marketing hooks are also helpful to mention in a query letter as well as during your pitch, as they cut to the heart of the story and tip off an editor as to the elements of your writing most likely to appeal to their readership.

Katherine Garbera is a bestselling author of Silhouette Desire novels and her Athena Force series helped launch its Bombshell line. In 'Making the Most of Your Editor/ Agent Appointment', she recommends using tags to describe your characters, such as 'single mom', 'Italian construction worker', etc. so the editor doesn't have to remember character names. Before coming to the appointment, Garbera says you should spend time working out your characters' goals, motivations and conflict. 'What does he/she want? (Goal), Why does he/she want it? (Motivation), and why can't he/she have it? (Conflict).' For your plot, 'How do they break apart? How do they get back together?'

Ten-point plan

Multi-award winning author of six Superromances, Linda Style (2003) has created a 10-point plan for pitching your book to an editor:

1. Think of your editor appointment as you would a job interview. You are selling yourself as well as your book. Dress professionally.
2. Smile, introduce yourself, shake hands, and if you have a card, offer it to the editor. (Some writers list the book they are pitching on the back side.)
3. If you have time for brief chit-chat that could break the ice, go for it. 'I attended your workshop. It was great . . .'
4. Tell the editor what type of book you've written

(contemporary/historical/paranormal), the title and length. Also mention the targeted line. A finished book carries more weight than an unfinished book, so if it's done, say so. If you've completed several others also say so, but pitch only one book unless the editor asks about others. If the editor says your book isn't right for her house, pitch another, or be prepared to ask lots of questions.

5. Go for the hook. Tell the editor whether it's a secret baby, amnesia, marriage of convenience, woman in jeopardy book and indicate the tone—light, dark, dramatic, comedic, etc. Tell the editor what makes your secret baby book different than the rest.

6. Give a brief one paragraph synopsis of the book that contains the main characters' goal, motivation, conflict and resolution. Practice this at home before the interview. Don't give too many details. For practice at home, start with the basics—the external conflict. Eloise wants (goal) ____, because (motivation) ____, but (conflict) ____. The conflict is resolved when ____. Then expand on this with a character tag. (A cynical cop wants ____.) The character tags can identify potential internal conflict/differences.

7. The editor may ask questions. Be prepared to answer. Don't go on so long you forget the time. If you can fit it in, give a little information about yourself and what makes you qualified to write the book. For example: if you're writing about law enforcement and you're an undercover cop, say so. If you're finished before your time is up, be prepared to ask a few questions of your own.

8. If the editor hasn't already asked to see the manuscript or a partial, close out the interview by asking if the editor would like to see yours.

9. Offer a friendly goodbye, handshake and a smile.
10. Send the editor a thank you note within a few days.

Questions to ask

If time allows and you have the chance to ask questions, or if you have no specific project to pitch at that time, author Katherine Garbera offers these suggestions:

For agents:
♥ What is your relationship with Silhouette (or whatever house you are interested in selling to)?
♥ What is your process with your clients? Specifically, when do you return calls? How long does it take you to turn around a project once it's submitted? Do you give creative input?
♥ What can you do to 'grow' an author?
♥ What are your expectations of an author and what can she expect in return from you?

For editors:
♥ Your tip sheet says that you like to grow authors (Silhouette's does), how do you do this?
♥ Though this project features a cowboy hero/ romantic comedy premise, etc I have other projects that don't. Will this be a problem?
♥ I notice Silhouette does a lot of special series in their lines. Are these closed to new authors or can I submit an idea to one of them?
♥ I really love to read your line and these authors are my favourites (only say this if it's true and you've actually read a book recently that you can name title and author). This isn't a question, more of a tip, but it can show an editor that you've done your research.

In group appointments, Katherine recommends sitting in the middle of the group to '. . . get an idea of what works for the agent/editor I'm pitching to. I can watch the way he/she reacts to the writer who has already pitched, and adjust my pitch accordingly.'

A pitch can be practised at home, or with a critique partner or group, and makes a useful creative writing exercise for you to try. Being able to break down your proposed novel to a paragraph of essential information is great practice for writing query letters, and later for handling media interviews when your book is published (thinking positive). As Linda Style concludes, 'With a little advance planning, you'll be able to walk into that interview with confidence and walk out with a request to submit your manuscript.'

10

To market, to market

*Y*ou've created a cast of memorable characters and a page-turning storyline. Where do you go from here? The answer is, 'to market'. Writing is a transaction which is not complete until someone reads your work. So where do you look for markets? This chapter lists some of the romance publishers and their basic requirements. A complete list can be found in the various writers' market guides that are published annually.

As well as complying with the guidelines set out in the publishers' tip sheets, your manuscript should be double spaced, with generous margins all around. Use good quality white paper and number every page in sequence. Don't start each new chapter with page one. Each chapter should start about halfway down the page. At the top of every page, put the book title or an abbreviated version of it, your name and the page number, in case the pages become separated.

The most commonly used fonts are Courier, Courier New or Times New Roman. You can use other fonts provided they are easy on the eye, but those listed are becoming publishing industry standard. Don't justify the right-hand margins. While some writers prefer to set italicised words in italic font, you may prefer to indicate italics by underlining words in the manuscript, so they are easier for an editor or typesetter to spot. More specific formatting requirements will depend on the individual publisher's house style.

The title page should show the book title, author's name, pen-name if used, your (or your agent's) contact numbers, and approximate word count. The manuscript should not be bound in any way. Most publishers prefer the loose sheets to be secured by two large elastic bands at right angles to each other.

A first-rate novel is unlikely to be rejected because you do any of these things differently, but in a competitive market it makes sense to present your work as well as you possibly can.

How to do a word count

Publishers usually specify the length of manuscript they require. This may vary from 50 000 words (the length of a Harlequin Presents or Silhouette romance novel) to 100 000 or more for chick lit and single-title books.

For most publishers, a reasonable estimate of length is acceptable. To arrive at this, use the same computer font throughout the manuscript. Use the same number of lines per page, the standard being 25 lines. Then count the number of words in several full lines of typing. Divide this number by the number of lines you have counted to give an average word count per line, then multiply the result by the number of lines per page. Count any half-pages and the first pages of chapters separately and add them to the first total to arrive at a reasonably accurate word count.

It's not advisable to rely on your computer word count as it calculates words differently to the averaging method used by most publishers (see above). In *Word Processing Secrets for Writers* Michael Banks and Ansen Dibell say that computer word counts can be as much as 20 per cent higher than counts using the traditional averaging method. This is because chapter headings, short-page chapter endings and so on can make a big difference. They solve the problem by taking the computer's character count and dividing it by six, rather than five, which is the number of characters in an 'average' word.

Whichever method you use, be sure to submit a manuscript which is as close as possible to the length required by the publisher. If it is appreciably longer or shorter, you risk automatic rejection.

There is no 'correct' chapter length. Around sixteen printed pages would be the chapter length of most of my short contemporary romances. This is about 4000 words. Although there are no hard and fast rules, there are usually around ten to twelve chapters to a 50 000-word manuscript. It's perfectly acceptable to have more chapters, but having fewer than ten may make each chapter too long for comfortable reading. Think of each chapter as an episode. When the episode ends, so should the chapter. If you are writing longer books, you will have many more chapters.

Although both are entirely optional, a prologue and/or an epilogue may be included in short romances. Both are usually shorter than the average chapter length, and sometimes are only a page or two. The prologue heightens the reader's anticipation, either by showing events that took place some time before the main story, or foreshadowing some major problem which will confront the hero or heroine as the book opens. An epilogue is found most commonly at the end of a book that is part of a series, to introduce the next book. It may also add a sense of completion to the main story, for example, by showing the couple living happily with their children. A prologue or an epilogue should always add something extra to the main story, not just make it longer.

The professional approach

Writing is a profession like any other. If you opened a café, you'd need to spend money on equipment, rental of premises, staffing and legal requirements before you even get to food and drink. Yet, because writing needs only a work surface, a chair and a computer, other equally important requirements are often overlooked. For example, what about bookkeeping? You must keep track of all writing-related income and expenses in a form acceptable to the taxation office, in order to claim deductions against writing income. What about marketing?

Editorial requirements change constantly and the only way to keep abreast of them is to read trade publications and belong to writers' groups. You can learn a great deal by attending workshops and conferences. Writers' centres in most states conduct these as well as providing members with up-to-date information. The Australian Society of Authors can advise you on contracts, copyright, fees you may be entitled to if your work is extensively photocopied by libraries or educational institutions, and Public Lending Right (a fee paid by government to writers to compensate for sales lost through their books being freely available in libraries).

Writers' organisations in Australia and overseas

Romance Writers of Australia
PO Box 37
Somerton Vic 3062

Telephone (03) 9305 4280
www.romanceaustralia.com

The Australian Society of Authors Ltd
PO Box 1566
Strawberry Hills NSW 2012
Telephone (02) 9318 0877
www.asauthors.org

Fellowship of Australian Writers (FAW)
PO Box 3036
Ripponlea Vic 3183
Telephone/Fax (03) 9528 7088
www.writers.asn.au

International PEN
Australian PEN Centres
C/- Melbourne PEN Centre
PO Box 2273
Caulfield Junction Vic 3161

The Society of Women Writers NSW Inc.
GPO Box 1388
Sydney NSW 2001
www.womenwritersnsw.org

Romance Writers of America (RWA)
1600 Stuebner Airline Drive
Suite 140
Spring TX 77379 USA
Telephone 832-717-5200
Fax 832-717-5201
www.rwanational.org

Romance Writers of America Australian Chapter
WBC Fletcher Jones Gardens
Warrnambool Vic 3280
Telephone (03) 5560 5054
Fax (03) 5560 5166
www.geocities.com/ausromance

Romance Writers of New Zealand Inc.
PO Box 64–311
Botany Town Centre
Maunkau City New Zealand
www.romancewriters.co.nz

The Romantic Novelists' Association UK
38 Stanhope Road
Reading Berkshire RG2 7HN UK
www.rna-uk.org

Magazines and websites of interest to romance writers

The Australian Author (journal of the Australian Society of Authors, available to nonmembers by subscription)

Hearts Talk (journal of Romance Writers of Australia)

Ozlit
PO Box 8094
Oakleigh East Vic 3166
www.home.vicnet.net.au/~ozlit/
Email: ozlit@netspace.net.au
A searchable database of authors, publishers' links and online reviews.

Romance Writers Report (journal of Romance Writers of America)

Romancing Australia (journal of Romance Writers of America Australian Chapter)

Romantic Times Book Club
55 Bergen Street
Brooklyn New York NY 11201 USA
www.romantictimes.com

www.literarymarketplace.com
Described as 'the world's largest, most complete database of the book publishing industry' with listings for publishers and literary agents in the United States, Canada and international. Access is by subscription, with some free pages available.

Writer's Digest Magazine
Box 2123
Harlan Iowa 51593 USA
www.writersdigest.com

The Writer Inc.
120 Boyleston Street
Boston MA 02116 USA
www.writermag.com

Critique services

Occasionally, critique services, also known as manuscript appraisal services, are advertised in authors' publications. Some publishers now say they will not look at manuscripts unless the author is represented by an agent or the work has been solicited by the publisher or favourably reviewed by a reputable manuscript appraisal service.

Lynk Manuscript Assessment Service grew out of the National Book Council's Assessment Service after that body closed in 1998. One of the convenors, Liat Kirby, continued the service in her own right, and it is recommended by publishers as a means of honing your work ready for publication. The author of *Curving My Eyes to Almonds*, Liat was administrator of the National Book Council, and a freelance reviewer for the *Australian Book Review* and the *Sydney Morning Herald*.

Liat says a writer's work 'doesn't stand a chance if they send it out under strength'. Her intent is to offer a detached and objective assessment of the work's strengths and weaknesses, and an insight into how the publishing industry works. She says she works with a team of experienced assessors, and only entrusts a manuscript to someone who has an understanding and appreciation of the specific genre. Fees and conditions are obtainable from Lynk at PO Box 174, Brunswick, Victoria 3056, www.lynkmas@vicnet.com.au.

Another agency recommended by publishers is The Manuscript Appraisal Agency (MAA) run by former HarperCollins publisher, Brian Cook, an industry insider for 33 years. As well as assisting writers with the editorial side of their work, Brian says he helps clients to 'get inside publishers, heads' so they understand an editor's likely response to their work.

The MAA does not publish or edit manuscripts, but Brian says it gives a commercial evaluation of content and advice as to how to get the manuscript to a standard acceptable by literary agents and publishers. Conditions and scale of fees are obtainable from PO Box 577, Terrigal NSW 2260, email briancook@manuscriptagency.com.au.

The Romance Writers (RW) of Australia, through its *Hearts Talk* newsletter, offers marketing information, how-to advice and fellowship among romance writers. RW Australia convenes online email groups and face-to-face groups throughout Australia, and provides a one-on-one mentoring scheme for isolated writers. All these are accessible by contacting the organisation.

The Australian chapter of Romance Writers of America runs workshops, conferences and provides information through the *Romancing Australia* newsletter.

In addition, most writers' centres conduct workshops on aspects of the craft which can be helpful, even if not specifically aimed at romance writing. You can even do writing courses on the Internet, such as those offered by *Writer's Digest* magazine, at:

www.writersonlineworkshops.com.

International manuscript appraisals

Probationary (unpublished) members of the English Romantic Novelists' Association are required to submit one manuscript a year for professional evaluation. The American *Romantic Times Book Club* offers a manuscript appraisal service and will look at anything from a query letter to a full manuscript. Contact the address given for its current rates, quoted in American dollars. I have seen some of its appraisals and they are thorough and helpful, especially if you plan to submit to the American market.

If you are a Canadian or American resident you can use the critique services offered by Harlequin Enterprises, where new writers may submit a partial or full manuscript for appraisal by an editor with extensive experience in the romance field. Manuscripts do not have to be aimed at lines published by Harlequin. Fees and conditions are obtainable from The Romance Novel Critiquing Service, 225 Duncan Mill Road, 4th floor, Don Mills, Ontario, Canada M3B 3K9 or from the publisher's website, www.eHarlequin.com.

Gaining expert editorial feedback is a great learning tool and a quick way to have your work seen by someone in the industry. Another way to progress is to find a critique partner to help and encourage you, while you do the same for them. It helps to have compatible writing interests and goals, and a working familiarity with the sub-genre your work is intended for. Critique partners or small groups of four to six partners can work face to face, by mail or, more commonly these days, by email.

Many of the larger organisations such as Romance Writers of America also have subgroups geared to the needs of writers interested in a particular setting or plot elements. Among such groups are The Beau Monde, for writers of romances set during England's Regency period; Espan, with the focus on electronic and small press publishers; Faith, Hope & Love, the outreach chapter for writers of inspirational romances; and Kiss of Death, where romance meets crime.

Contests

These are an excellent way of honing your writing skills, escaping the infamous slush pile of unsolicited manuscripts and bringing your work to the attention of editors at major publishing houses. The Australian chapter of Romance

Writers of America paid me a great compliment when they established the Valerie Parv Award in my honour. Open to authors unpublished in romance fiction, the award is for the first three chapters (or prologue and two chapters), plus a two-page single-spaced synopsis of your novel. Eligible categories include contemporary romance, romances with paranormal, horror, fantasy or time-travel elements, medical themes and books aimed at single-title romance lines. Currently, I mentor the winner for the year of their award, and their entry is critiqued by a senior romance editor. For periodical updates see www.valerieparv.com.

Entry into the Emma Darcy Award is restricted to members of Romance Writers of Australia, but is an excellent motivation to finish a book and have it read by an acquiring editor. Many entrants over the past ten years have succeeded in a variety of writing fields including literary fiction. Previous finalists and winners who have been published by Harlequin Silhouette include Bronwyn Jameson, Fiona Brand, Laura Ruch, Melissa James, Nalini Singh, Ris Wilkinson and Trish Morey. *Hearts Talk* editor, Paula Roe, cites 'editor feedback, a sense of accomplishment, accolades and a huge feeling of self-worth' as benefits of entering. Current information is available from www.romanceaustralia.com or from Romance Writers of Australia.

A number of competitions are run each year by Romance Writers of New Zealand (RWNZ) and its sponsors. The Clendon Award was established by Barbara and Peter Clendon, owners of specialist romance bookshop, Barbara's Books. This contest enables entrants to obtain feedback from a panel of dedicated romance readers. Finalists then have their work sent to New York to be judged by a top romance editor. A full manuscript is required, with the closing date usually in February each year, and results announced at an annual conference normally held in August. RWNZ also conducts a first meeting/synopsis competition, with finalists having their work judged by an editor at Harlequin Mills & Boon, London. Contest details can be obtained from the RWNZ or at www.romancewriters.co.nz.

According to its website, Romance Writers of America (RWA) created the Golden Heart Awards to 'honour the work of unpublished (writers) and bring their work to the attention of the publishing community'. Entry is open to members, nonmembers and collaborators, provided the manuscript is not under offer from a publisher and the entrant is not published by a RWA-recognised publisher. This means authors published by most small presses and the majority of e-publishers may remain eligible. Entrants submit a partial, maximum 55 pages double spaced. The synopsis may be single spaced. However, you sign a declaration that you have completed the manuscript and this is verified by random checking. Entries are read by five judges in the preliminary round, with the final round being judged by romance editors. Details are announced at www.rwanational.org and in *Romance Writers Report*. Entries close in December and winners are announced at RWA's annual conference each northern summer.

To help defray costs, an entry fee is charged for most competitions run by writers' organisations.

From time to time, magazines and major publishers run contests open to new writers. This is a good way to polish your work for publication, meet deadlines and showcase your book to editors. For several years, Dorchester Publishing has sponsored a New Voice contest for unpublished authors in conjunction with *Romantic Times Book Club*, with the chance to gain a one-book contract. Typically, the contest is announced in March, with entries due in June and the winner chosen in October. The winning book is published the following July. The category of romance varies by year and has included historicals, paranormals, time travel and futuristics. Details of current requirements can be obtained by contacting the publisher or www.dorchesterpub.com.

In addition, most writing organisations run contests focusing on specific aspects of the craft. Many are judged by published writers or editors, at least in the final stages. The most valuable are those providing a score sheet showing you how the judges rated various aspects of your entry. Remember that these scores are subjective, reflecting the opinions of one person, so try not to be disheartened if your work receives a low score. For every person who dislikes an aspect, some other judge may score it more highly. However, if the responses are consistent and cite similar reasons for the low scores, it could be worth paying attention to these points in future.

Some frequent queries answered

Harlequin Mills & Boon receives thousands of unsolicited manuscripts every year and gives the following answers to the most frequently asked questions concerning manuscript submission:

How do I know which series to write for?
By reading books in each series you'll find a series you like best. This is the one you should write for.

Do you really read every submission?
Yes. Because of the large number of submissions we receive, however, our response time to each submission varies.

What is an international postal coupon?
If you have sent your manuscript to a foreign country—from the United Kingdom to Canada for example—you'll need to enclose international postage coupons for the return of your manuscript. If your post office does not carry IPCs and you would like to have your manuscript returned, enclose a cheque for the proper amount of return postage.

Do I need an agent?
Harlequin Enterprises works with authors who are, and authors who are not represented by agents.

How do I know that Harlequin Enterprises has received my manuscript?
Please include a self-addressed postcard, either stamped or with IPC, with the manuscript delivery.

What are some things you can do to help sell your manuscript?
First, we expect you to enjoy reading romance fiction. If you are already a fan, your appreciation of this type of book will be apparent in the writing. If you have not done so already, we encourage you to read many, many books from each series. The series that emerges as your favourite is probably where you should submit your manuscript.

Secondly, remember that reading is an emotional experience. We hope you will write from the heart and we will feel touched by what you have to say. When you put pen to paper (or finger to keyboard), do so because you have something to share with other readers.

Romance-friendly publishers

Avalon Books
160 Madison Avenue, New York, NY 10016, USA
Publishes four hardcover contemporary romances plus two historical romances and two westerns every second month, plus two mysteries every two months. Seeks 'wholesome adult fiction' with no explicit sex. Word length from 40 000 to 60 000 words. Submit query letter with synopsis and first three sample chapters. Query by mail only, no submissions on disk.

Avon Books
10 E 53rd Street, New York, NY 10022, USA
Email: avonromance@harpercollins.com
Publishes contemporary and historical romances, romantic suspense, African-American. Prefers email query with a two-page description of your book. What is the setting? Contemporary or historical? Who are the hero and heroine, and what happens to them? Do not send a longer synopsis, sample chapters or manuscript until requested, but do have material available to send quickly if required.

Ballantine/Ivy
1745 Broadway, 18th Floor, New York, NY 10019, USA
www.ballantinebooks.com
Suggests you read their list online to ascertain current requirements, primarily 'big' romances, heavy on plot. No guidelines available. Unagented writers should query first, then send 50-page partial on request. No dot matrix, disk or email submissions.

The Bantam Dell Publishing Group
1745 Broadway, New York, NY 10019, USA
Only accepts agented material, no unsolicited or email submissions. No specific guidelines available.

Barbour Publishing Inc. & Heartsong Presents
PO Box 719, Uhrichsville, OH 44683, USA
Email: fictionsubmit@barbourbooks.com
Publishes inspirational romances, two contemporary and two historical per month. Seeking well-rounded stories with characters of strong Christian principles, especially African-American, Asian and/or Hispanic, as well as traditional romances including mysteries where characters are guided by their faith. General guidelines available online or by sending a stamped self-addressed envelope (SSAE). Send synopsis and three sample chapters by mail or email; no unsolicited full manuscripts or disk submissions.

Belle Books
PO Box 67, Smyrna, GA 30081, USA
www.bellebooks.com
Seeking short stories for anthologies set in the fictional Southern town of Mossy Creek. Stories must relate to existing material. Check the website for details, then send one-page query by email to MossyEditorial@aol.com.

Berkeley/Jove
375 Hudson Street, New York, NY 10014, USA
Publishes contemporary, historical, paranormal, romantic suspense and single-title mainstream romances of 100 000 words under Jove and Berkeley imprints. Seeks two- to five-page synopsis and first three chapters. Finished manuscript should be available. General guidelines available

with a SSAE. New and established writers considered. No computer disk or email submissions.

BET Books/Arabesque
Office of the Publisher
555 West 57th Street, 11th Floor,
New York, NY, 10019, USA
www.bet.com
Publishes four contemporary genre novels of 85 000 to 100 000 words per month under the Arabesque line; also launching into mainstream women's fiction under the Sepia imprint, and inspirational fiction under the New Spirit imprint, both lines 90 000 to 100 000 words. All lines feature non-Caucasian (predominantly African-American) characters and are aimed at a mainly middle-class readership. For Arabesque, sub-genre elements such as mystery, adventure and humour are welcome as long as they don't overshadow the romance. Sepia novels should feature genre plots such as suspense-driven thrillers, mystery/adventure and books that explore the bonds of sisterhood and relationship, offering a realistic view of urban life. New Spirit books feature contemporary issues and strong characters who overcome obstacles through the power of prayer and faith. This imprint will also offer nonfiction books of 70 000 to 90 000 words to encourage and motivate readers. Send a query letter briefly explaining the nature of the story and mentioning any previous publishing credits, plus a two- or three-page detailed synopsis and first three chapters. No computer materials or handwritten work.

Dorchester Publishing
200 Madison Avenue, Suite 2000, New York,
NY 10016 USA

www.dorchesterpub.com
Publishes eleven Leisure Books and four Love Spells per
month. Seeking contemporary, historical, time-travel,
futuristic and paranormal romances of 90 000 to 100 000
words. No romantic suspense or category-length manuscripts. Also seeking contemporary and present-day
paranormals of 45 000 words for the young adult Smooch
line, aimed at girls aged 12–16. Submission guidelines
available on the web or by mail. Basically, submit a query,
or synopsis and three sample chapters written from third
person viewpoint. Open to unsolicited manuscripts and
unagented authors. No bound manuscripts, multiple submissions, dot matrix printing or computer disks.

Echelon Press
PO Box 1084, Crowley, TX 76036, USA
Publisher of e-books in single-title (50 000 to 120 000
words) and short story/novella (6000 to 50 000 words) for
downloading. Seeking general fiction, adventure, thrillers,
mystery/suspense, paranormal, western, ultra-sensual and
young adult. Guidelines available on the web or by mail.
Seeks cover letter with introduction and writing credits,
brief synopsis and word count, plus hard copy of first
three chapters of novels, or entire manuscript for novellas,
plus disk in .rtf or .doc format. No email submissions
considered.

Ellora's Cave
PO Box 787, Hudson, OH 44236–0787, USA
www.ellorascave.com
Established as an electronic publisher, now with wide
paperback distribution, this is the first e-publisher recognised by Romance Writers of America as eligible to enter

its RITA awards. This recognition depends on a minimum track record and minimum book sales set by RWA. Books are published in both electronic and trade or mass market paperback format of 35 000 to 40 000 words, and 25 000-word novellas. Categories include contemporary, fantasy, futuristic, historical, not-so-Grimm fairytales, romantic suspense and paranormals. All manuscripts must contain sexual content varying in strength according to the publisher's rating system. Erotica without romance is not considered. See guidelines on the web for other restrictions. Submit a synopsis and first three to four chapters electronically as a Word or Rich text files via the website.

Harlequin Books, Canada
225 Duncan Mill Road, Don Mills, Ontario, Canada
M3B 3K9
www.eHarlequin.com
Publishes six Superromances per month, four Temptations, two Flipside romantic comedies (witty 65 000-word books replacing the Duets 2-in-1 line), and four 'sexy, sizzling' Blaze novels. Guidelines available for all lines by mail or on the web. Query first with a cover letter and short synopsis to the appropriate editor listed in the guidelines, then submit a detailed synopsis and sample chapters if requested. Submissions are open to new authors, whether agented or not. No multiple submissions, dot matrix printing or computer disks.

Harlequin Books, New York
233 Broadway, Suite 1001, 10th floor, New York,
NY 10279, USA
www.eHarlequin.com
Publishes four Harlequin American Romances, four

Intrigue and four Historicals per month. Guidelines for all Harlequin lines available with SSAE or on the web. 'Actively seeking' new authors for American Romance and Intrigues. Traditional themes of secret babies, single mothers, amnesia plots and single fathers are welcome, but avoid non-selling content such as actors or theatre backgrounds, treasure hunts, espionage and issues-oriented plots, e.g. save the whales. For Intrigue, romantic suspense should involve the hero and heroine on a personal level, the action bringing them closer together. Prefers authors to query first with a cover letter and short synopsis.

Harlequin Mills & Boon Ltd, United Kingdom
Eton House, 18–24 Paradise Road, Richmond, Surrey TW9 1SR, UK
www.millsandboon.co.uk
Publishes eighteen contemporary romances, including six contemporary medical romances of 50 000 to 55 000 words and two historical romances per month. Guidelines available. Prefers a one- to two-page synopsis and first three chapters. Open to unsolicited submissions and un-agented writers. No multiple submissions, dot matrix printing or computer disks. Include sufficient international postage coupons for reply only or return of submission (state which you prefer).

Harlequin's Australasian marketing office has writers' guidelines (but no editorial advice). Contact 8 Gibbes, Street Chatswood NSW 2067 or www.eHarlequin. com.au.

Harvest House
990 Owen Loop North, Eugene, OR 97402, USA
Looking for sweet Christian contemporary romances with enough conflict to sustain reader interest and touch lives

without being message-driven. Query first. Authors need not be agented.

HQN Books
233 Broadway, Suite 1001, New York, NY 10279, USA
www.eHarlequin.com
A Harlequin imprint, debuting in 2004 for single-title mainstream novels in mass market and trade paperback size with romance as the central element, around 100 000 words. Can contain a wide variety of fictional elements, such as suspense, provided the romance remains the primary focus. Agented and unagented writers and simultaneous submissions welcome. Guidelines available on the web or by mail.

ImaJinn Books
PO Box 545, Canon City, CO 81215-0545, USA
www.imajinnbooks.com
Publishes 24 to 30 romances per year featuring supernatural, futuristic or fantasy elements, as well as a new erotic–paranormal romance line for release initially as e-books only. Looking for specific storylines to fill available slots, so writers should check the website for current requirements. Also publishes a children's line which is not currently seeking submissions. Guidelines available on the web or by mail. Welcomes unagented and first-time authors. Query first before submitting manuscripts. Previously e-published books no longer considered.

Kensington Publishing Group
850 Third Avenue, New York, NY 10022, USA
www.kensingtonbooks.com
Publishes more than 500 new books per year under Zebra, Pinnacle and Citadel imprints, including contemporary

and historical romances, Regency, alternative and bilingual (English–Spanish) romances. Submissions only accepted via literary agents. Some guidelines available on the web or by mail. Send cover letter and detailed three- to five-page synopsis. When a project is solicited, published authors should send synopsis, first three chapters or full manuscript and a copy of their previous book; new authors must submit full manuscript. Include return postage or give permission to recycle materials. Letter-quality printing required; no disks or unsolicited material considered.

LUNA Books
233 Broadway, Suite 1001, 10th floor, New York, NY 10279, USA
www.eHarlequin.com
Emotionally complex female fantasy novels of 100 000 to 150 000 words set in other worlds, both alternate histories and contemporary. Romantic subplots enhance the story but don't become the focus. First, third or multiple viewpoints accepted but strong heroine predominates. Guidelines available. Submit detailed synopsis and three sample chapters or complete manuscript.

MIRA Books
225 Duncan Mill Road, Don Mills, Ontario, Canada M3B 3K9
www.Mirabooks.com
Commercial fiction of 100 000 words plus, ranging from contemporary relationship stories to romantic suspense, psychological thrillers and family sagas published in hardcover, original trade and mass market paperbacks. Submissions accepted from agented authors only and consisting of a synopsis and first two chapters.

Multnomah Publishers
204 W Adams Avenue, PO Box 1720, Sisters,
OR 97759, USA
www.multnomahbooks.com
Publishes 25 novels a year from 85 000 to 100 000 words, promoting a biblical worldview without preaching. Characters should be believable and likable, and undergo change as they face difficulties and make choices consistent with evangelical Christian principles. Guidelines available on the web or by mail. Queries accepted through agents or following contact with editors at writers' conferences, when you should send a cover letter, synopsis and at least three sample chapters. No email submissions or reprints accepted.

New American Library (NAL)
375 Hudson Street, New York, NY 10014, USA
www.penguinputnam.com
Publishes three Signet Regency romances per month, as well as Signet historicals and mainstream contemporary women's fiction under Signet, Onyx and Accent imprints. Currently seeking submissions for all lines. Mainstream women's suspense, romantic suspense, chick lit and 'lady lit' also welcome. No guidelines available. Prefers writers to be agented. Unagented authors should submit query to a specific editor and include a return address and a SSAE. No unsolicited manuscripts or partials, email submissions, dot matrix printing or computer disks.

Pocket Books
1230 Avenue of the Americas, New York, NY 10020, USA
www.simonsays.com
Publishes single-title contemporary and historical romances,

chick lit, erotica and sexy romances, humorous historicals, African-American romances and women's fiction. Looking for both published authors and new voices. Submit a query letter, first three chapters and a SSAE for response. Computer disks not accepted.

Random House Australia
20 Alfred Street, Milsons Point NSW 2061, Australia
www.randomhouse.com.au
Publishes a wide range of fiction including science fiction, fantasy, popular fiction, literary novels and romance. Unsolicited submissions accepted only from previously published authors, agents and writers with positive assessments from a reputable manuscript appraisal agency. Find these through writers' centres or organisations such as the Australian Society of Authors. Queries should be hard copy only and include a cover letter, synopsis, author CV and first three chapters or 50 manuscript pages. No email or digital submissions or disks.

Red Dress Ink
C/- M. Marbury 233 Broadway, 10th floor, New York, NY 10279, USA
C/- K. Lye, 225 Duncan Mill Road, Don Mills, Ontario M3B3K9, Canada
C/- S. Bell, Eton House, 18–24 Paradise Road, Richmond, Surrey TW9 1SR, UK
www.RedDressInk.com
Modern women's fiction of 80 000 to 110 000 words featuring a strong female protagonist and concerns relevant to modern 20-something readers. Not only chick lit, but 'women's fiction with attitude'. Submit a detailed synopsis

and three sample chapters or the complete manuscript to Red Dress Ink at one of the three acquiring offices listed.

Red Sage Publishing
PO Box 4844, Seminole, FL 33775, USA
www.redsagepub.com
Publishes Secrets anthologies of adult romances between 25 000 to 40 000 words, concentrating on the love and sexual relations between hero and heroine. Described as bold, spicy, untamed and sometimes politically incorrect, they still end happily. Send query with a one-page synopsis highlighting the emotional and physical conflict in your story and first ten printed pages of manuscript. Unpublished authors welcome. Send a SSAE for return of manuscript. No multiple submissions, dot matrix printing, computer disks or email submissions.

Rocky River Romance/Saltwater Press
PO Box 535, Merrylands NSW 2160, Australia
www.rockyriverromance.com
Email: enquiries@rockyriver.com
An independent Australian press with international distribution. Publishes 55 000- to 60 000-word historical and contemporary romances of 'scenery, substance and sex' reflecting the ideals of modern Australian women. Any Australian backgrounds and historical periods considered, as well as styles from classic romance to literary works. Guidelines available on the web or by mail. Prefers emailed query in first instance introducing the author and why story is considered special, plus 1000-word synopsis detailing setting, lead characters, plot, conflict and resolution, and word count. When mailing requested material, send a SSAE for return or allow material to be recycled if unsuitable.

Silhouette Books
233 Broadway, Suite 1001, 10th floor, New York, NY 10279, USA
www.eHarlequin.com
Publishes four Silhouette Romances, six Desire titles (short, sensual), six Special Editions (sensual, contemporary), six Intimate Moments (longer, action-oriented romances) and the latest Silhouette Bombshell line (100 000-words-plus heroine-driven action—adventure novels with romance as a lesser element). All Silhouette editors read and acquire for all lines. Guidelines available from the senior editor of each line or on the web. Read widely to identify the distinctive tone of each line. Editors are eager to see traditional plot elements handled in fresh ways within each line's individual character. Writers are encouraged to find their own voices and may write for more than one line while working with the same editor. Query first with covering letter and two-page synopsis. Unpublished writers welcome. No fax or email submissions, dot matrix printing or computer disks.

St. Martin's Press
175 Fifth Avenue, New York, NY 10010, USA
www.stmartins.com
Publishes all kinds of commercial women's fiction (other than category length), 100 000- to 120 000-word historicals set in various time periods, suspense and paranormal. Open to more Scottish, medieval and Regency-set historicals (no straight Regencies), sexy paranormals and modern romantic comedies, all from 90 000 to 120 000 words. No guidelines or tip sheets available. Send query letter, but no manuscripts or partials until requested. No email queries or computer disks.

Steeple Hill Books
233 Broadway, Suite 1001, 10th floor, New York, NY 10279, USA
www.eHarlequin.com
Publishes four Love Inspired contemporary romances per month from 70 000 to 75 000 words with the power of faith integrated into characters and plot. Wants vivid, exciting romances (no explicit sex), which may include children and touches of mystery, drama, humour. Also seeking quality inspirational women's fiction detailing the struggles of Christians in modern or historical settings. These 80 000- to 125 000-word books can focus on more complex stories in various sub-genres from family dramas to relationship novels, Christian chick lit, suspense, romantic suspense, medical and legal thrillers. Generally, sensuality and sexual desire are kept to a minimum, and references to specific Christian denominations should be avoided. Guidelines available by mail or on the web. Query first with cover letter and two-page synopsis. Open to unagented and first-time writers. No faxes or computer disks.

Tor/Forge
Tom Doherty Associates LLC, 175 Fifth Avenue, New York, NY 10010, USA
www.tor.com
Looking for well-researched historical fiction set in any time or place (preferably not Victorian/Edwardian urban settings), mysteries with strong female protagonists, romantic novel-length stories with paranormal elements including more erotic stories, non-traditional romances crossing cultural, ethnic, religious and gender divides, as well as traditional romances with more complex, multi-layered plots; 80 000 to 130 000 words. A thinking heroine

who is active in solving her problems is desired. Mysteries must be genuinely baffling and romances should not involve easily solved misunderstandings. Guidelines on the web at www.tor.com/torfaq.html. Paranormal guidelines at www.tor.com/paranormalromance.html or by mail. No queries by phone or fax.

Tyndale House
351 Executive Drive, Carol Stream, IL 60188, USA
www.heartquest.com
Publishes inspirational historical and contemporary romances under Heartquest, and inspirational mainstream women's fiction, all with strong Christian themes without preaching. Shows characters who rely on faith to overcome obstacles and attain a love to last a lifetime. Women's fiction is a woman's story told from her perspective, with varying degrees of romance, and may not end happily. Word range from 75 000 to 100 000. Also publishing anthologies of three 25 000-word novellas with a common theme. Guidelines on the web or by mail should be read before querying. Send cover letter with your introduction and writing history, hero and heroine's goals and conflict, and the Christian theme, with a one- to two-page synopsis and first three chapters. Include a SSAE if materials are to be returned. No dot matrix or disk submissions.

Warner Books
1271 Avenue of the Americas, New York, NY 10020, USA
www.twbookmark.com
Publishes two to three single-title contemporary and historical romances per month, preferably from agented authors, although queries from unagented authors will be reviewed. No guidelines available.

Warner Faith
10 Cadillac Drive, Suite 220, Brentwood, TN 37027, USA
www.twbookmark.com/christian
Publishing contemporary inspirational women's fiction from 70 000 to 90 000 words, and some general and more romantically based women's fiction. Open to all types, romantic, humorous, serious, heartfelt and mystery-based. Prefers to see series proposals rather than stand-alone titles. Submissions via agents only.

Zondervan
5300 Patterson Ave SE, Grand Rapids, MI 49530, USA
www.zondervan.com
Publishes various genres of inspirational fiction including traditional and mainstream romances of 85 000 to 90 000 words, but no science fiction or fantasy. Proposals of no more than five pages may be faxed to the publisher, but prefers that authors register submissions with the Evangelical Christian Publishers Association's First Edition website, www.ecpa.org/FE/. Book proposals on this website are reviewed by all members of the association, and Zondervan has assigned an editor to this task. No email proposals or unsolicited mail packages accepted.

Always include a stamped, self-addressed envelope (SSAE) when querying editors. If submitting to a foreign address, send the appropriate amount of return postage in international postal/reply coupons (IPCs or IRCs). Alternatively, you may advise the publisher that the manuscript can be recycled if it proves unsuitable. Keeping a copy can be more economical than supplying return postage.

11
Questions and answers

$\mathcal{M}$ ost of your writing-related questions will already have been addressed. However, there are always one or two questions lingering in people's minds. This, then, is 'question time'.

Do I need an agent to get accepted?
Having an agent won't guarantee acceptance, and it can be as difficult to gain an agent as a book contract. Many publishers say they will look at query letters from unagented writers, and will then invite proposals and manuscripts if your work catches their enthusiasm. Harlequin Mills & Boon goes as far as to say the offer you receive is the same whether you have an agent or not. I have sold books both with and without an agent, but before I was represented I taught myself to understand and negotiate contracts and deal effectively with publishers. You may prefer someone else to do this while you stick to writing. Since it's hard for a new writer to persuade an agent to represent you, it may be easier to market your book yourself initially, then invite an agent to negotiate the contract for you once you're accepted, and to act for you from then on.

Should I use a pen-name and who owns it if I do?
A pen-name protects your privacy, allows you to write different kinds of books without one type prejudicing the

other, and lets you write for more than one publisher without competing with yourself. Ownership depends on the terms of your contract. Make sure you don't sign away the right to a name you may wish to use elsewhere in the future. Some writers write under their maiden name, which is not strictly a pen-name. In the romance field, collaborators may write under a joint pen-name, but you should have a legal agreement setting out future use and ownership of the pen-name to protect both of you.

Do publishers read submissions? I've heard of writers sticking pages together which come back untouched.
Setting traps for editors is unprofessional. Harlequin Mills & Boon says it reads every submission with great care. I assume other publishers do the same. Remember, you don't need to eat a whole apple to know it's fresh. Editors can often tell from page one if a book has what they're looking for—that's why they're editors.

How much money can I make?
This is the question on everyone's lips. It's true that romance writing has made some authors millionaires, but more often it's a good to very good living. Six-figure incomes are possible, but allow three to five years of hard work before you see much return at all. Advances start from around $1000, to six figures or more for a mainstream single-title romance. Some publishers divide the advance between signing and publication, others pay part on acceptance of the manuscript and the balance on publication. Royalties are only payable after the book earns back its advance in sales. Some books barely break even, others earn considerably more than the advance, especially if they're translated into many languages. It is true that the best books earn the best returns.

If I submit a synopsis, will someone steal my idea?
Professional editors lack the time and inclination to steal
ideas. If they like your query, they'll encourage you to
develop it for them. Ideas cannot be copyrighted, only the
form in which they are presented. So two writers may
produce books on a Cinderella theme, say, and provided
the treatment of the ideas is original, this is perfectly
acceptable. Likewise, titles can't be copyrighted, so you
have *By Honour Bound* by Dorothy Cork (Silhouette),
Honour Bound by Laura Taylor (Berkeley), *By Honour
Bound* by Valerie Gray (a Regency romance from Leisure),
and *Honour Bound* by Jennifer Brassel (Rocky River
Romance).

I hate writing sex scenes. Are they obligatory?
To thine own self be true. Only write scenes you feel comfortable about but make sure you submit to a line which
agrees with your preferences. It's no use sending a sweet
romance to a publisher which has built a market for
spicy romances. Also, for most lines other than those
flagged as erotica, you should be writing 'love scenes'
rather than 'sex scenes'. There is a difference.

Must I introduce the hero on the first page?
In a short, category romance, the answer is yes, or as close
to the opening pages as possible. We should either meet
him, or be aware of his imminent impact (by having other
characters speculate about the new boss, for example) as
early in the book as possible. A romance requires two
people and the reader wants to see them get together. In
chick lit and single-title books, which are generally longer,
you have more flexibility.

If my outline is accepted, must I stick to it?
A synopsis is a guide, not a straitjacket. As long as the book is substantially the same as the one in your query or partial, no editor will hold you to the precise details. Characters change, storylines develop in new directions and editors know this. An outline should enhance your creativity, not stifle it.

Must I visit every place I write about?
If you can, terrific. In many cases, it may also be tax deductible. If you can't—historical writers and science fiction writers can't, after all—do extensive homework and check every little detail, then use your imagination.

How do I overcome 'blank page' syndrome, when I just don't know what to write?
Fear of the blank page, writer's block, whatever you call it, hits all writers sometimes. In my guide to creativity, *The Idea Factory*, I advocate simply sitting down and starting to write. Write foolish, idiotic nonsense. If you can, steer the nonsense along the general lines of your project. But begin. Give yourself permission to start in the middle or at the end. Don't stop to do more research, make coffee or even go to the bathroom. These urges come from your logical left brain which is trying to stay in charge. This is creative right-brain time. As Goethe is popularly but erroneously credited with saying, 'Whatever you can do or dream you can, begin it. Boldness has genius, power and magic in it.'

Appendix I
Sample writers' guidelines

*T*his is an example of the writers' guidelines—also called tip sheets—which publishers send on request to aspiring authors. This sample is for short category romances. To obtain current guidelines, visit the publisher's website where guidelines are often listed, or write to the publisher's mailing address, usually found in recent publications, and enclose sufficient return postage for the reply.

> A fine romance . . . is hard to find
>
> Editor seeks manuscripts for publication in women's Category Romance market. Applications should be between 50 000–55 000 words long and concerned with the development of true love (with view to marriage) between lady 17–28, and gentleman, 30–45 (must be rich and/or powerful). Exotic locations preferred, happy ending essential. Applications in writing to: Editorial Department, Romance Fiction, Mills & Boon Ltd, Eton House, 18–24 Paradise Road, Richmond, Surrey TW9 1SR, England.

If only it were as easy as that! Every Harlequin Mills & Boon reader and aspiring writer has a very clear picture of what makes our books so successful; some people have tried to reduce it to a formula which, in its essentials, would look very much like the fake ad above. But in order to keep up the high reputation which rests at the core of Harlequin Mills & Boon's success, we have to be a lot tougher than that.

We believe that the so-called formula is only the beginning, and that originality, imagination and individuality are the most important qualities in a romance writer. Any competent novelist can follow a detailed recipe for success, but we want writers who have the sort of star quality that makes their books instantly recognisable as *theirs*. The editorial office receives nearly 4000 manuscripts for consideration every year from aspiring authors. If a dozen new authors are selected for publication in that time, we reckon we are having a bumper year!

In a very short space of time, the world of romantic fiction has grown into a big business, and it's not easy to stay businesslike and *romantic*. However, we still believe that quality is more important than quantity—that romance readers deserve the best we can find. A book that simply 'makes the right noises' will *not* make a Harlequin Mills & Boon.

What do we look for when we read a manuscript for the first time? Many would-be authors have tried to find exactly the right note, but have had to admit defeat in the end. Surprisingly, we don't worry too much about flawless presentation; a book that has been written with genuine feeling can be forgiven a few typographical mistakes. What is more important is a genuine love of storytelling, combined with a freshness and originality of approach. Sincerity, and belief in the characters as real people, communicate themselves to the reader; if a writer is less concerned about conveying the heroine's innermost thoughts so that the reader understands and sympathises, than making sure the hero first kisses her on page 18 as laid down by the tip sheet, that preoccupation will show up on the page. Similarly, although imitation is the sincerest form of flattery, we don't want new authors whose work echoes the style of our readers' current favourites. Each of our authors must possess an individual touch, her own particular way of telling a story, and this quality is vital. The great artist is not simply someone who can paint a human figure with the right number of arms and legs, and the great musician does more than hit the correct notes in the correct order! In the same way, it is what a romance writer creates with her material that makes her book special (and successful); a good book is not simply a question of constructing a plot with a hero, a heroine, two quarrels and a happy ending, and spinning it out for 200 pages.

The story doesn't necessarily have to be complicated—in fact, a simple tale introducing only a few characters besides the hero and heroine is often very successful. Make sure, however, that the characters are convincing in both their actions and their words. If the hero is meant to be a man of authority, used to being obeyed, he should be shown as such and the other characters should react to him accordingly. With such clues of behaviour, too, it is not always necessary to state bald facts; you can afford to keep the reader guessing by stimulating his/her imagination. For instance, if you include a scene in which the heroine quarrels violently with someone, then there is no need to state that she has an unpredictable temper! If such behaviour is unusual, the reason for it (nervous strain, a headache, a feeling of apprehension) immediately gives the reader a deeper understanding of the heroine's character, and one that has been arrived at by guesswork; the reader who guesses about a character in a book is an interested reader. In general, the dialogue should be completely unstilted. A would-be writer should be aware of everyday patterns of speech, and should try to make the characters as true to life as possible.

Equally important is the background against which the principal characters are set. It is vital that this should be as accurate as research allows, although there is no substitute for an author's personal knowledge of a particular background. All Mills & Boon authors spend a good deal of time checking the material used in their books, because they realise how quickly the recognition of a fault or inaccuracy can spoil the reader's enjoyment of a scene.

This care should be extended to small details, as well as the more obvious points such as foreign locations and customs; if, for instance, a would-be writer has no idea about office life, it is a mistake to make the heroine a secretary! A working knowledge of the practical details is essential at such points. All this may sound like obvious common sense, but it is surprising how often the obvious is ignored!

When attempting a Mills and Boon novel, concentrate on writing a good book rather than a saleable proposition. A good book sells itself and is good indefinitely, while a 'saleable proposition' tends to be based on what is saleable *at the time of writing*—even if a publisher snaps it up, the world will have moved on by at least nine months by the time it finally appears. Think of what you, as a reader, would like to read, rather than what you think an editor will buy—the one will lead to the other if all goes well.

A Mills & Boon [short romance] has a standard length of about 190 printed pages—between 50 000 and 55 000 words. From a purely practical angle, any manuscript which differs so greatly that its author cannot reduce or expand its size to fit this requirement is unsuitable. The most important consideration in accepting or rejecting a manuscript is, however, whether the story lives up to the high standard that readers have set for us. We know from their letters what they like and dislike about our books, and their opinions matter to us. Maybe we can't please every one of our readers all the time, but it isn't for want of trying!

Appendix II
How to submit a novel

*H*ow to prepare your submission to Harlequin®, Silhouette®, Mills & Boon® and Steeple Hill®.

Unless otherwise noted, we do not accept unsolicited complete manuscripts, but ask instead that you submit a query letter. The query letter should include a word count, and pertinent facts about yourself as a writer including your familiarity with the romance genre and an outline of your story. Please indicate which series you are writing for, if it is completed, what you think makes it special, and previous publishing experience (if any). Also include a synopsis of your story that gives a clear idea of both your plot and character development, and is no more than two single-spaced pages. A self-addressed envelope and return international postage coupons will ensure a reply. Should your manuscript be requested, please note the following information.

1. Harlequin, Silhouette, Mills & Boon and Steeple Hill publish only category/series romances (and inspirational romances under Steeple Hill). Please do not submit any other type of fiction or non-fiction. Your manuscript should be told in the third person, primarily from the heroine's point of view. However, the hero's perspective may be used to enhance tension, plot

or character development. Please see the guidelines for further details of each series.

2. All material should be the author's own original work. Stories that contain scenes or plot lines that bear a striking resemblance to a previously published work are in breach of copyright laws and are not acceptable.

3. All material must be typewritten, double-spaced and on a reasonably heavy bond paper. No disk submissions. Computer-generated material is acceptable, but must be letter quality, and pages must be separated. Any material received on computer reams will be returned without evaluation.

4. Do not submit your material in binders, boxes or containers of any kind. Secure material by rubber bands. Cover sheets must have your complete name, address and phone number. Each page should be numbered sequentially thereafter. Please type your name and title in the left-hand corner of each page. If we ask to see your manuscript, please include a complete synopsis. Enclose a self-addressed, stamped postcard if you require acknowledgement of receipt.

5. All material will be evaluated in as timely a fashion as volume allows. Please do not call regarding the status of your manuscript. You will be notified by mail as soon as your work has been reviewed.

6. Do not send any material that is being considered by another publisher. Multiple submissions are not acceptable. A literary agent is not required in order to submit.

7. You must enclose a stamped, self-addressed envelope with all material that you send in. This will ensure return of your material. Please send an envelope large enough to accommodate your work and adequate

postage in the form of international postage coupons or an international money order where appropriate.

8. This sheet is designed as a guide to aid you in understanding our requirements and standards. However, there is no better way to determine what we are looking for than reading our books.

9. We enter into discussions about payment only when a contract is offered. This information is confidential.

10. We take every reasonable care of manuscripts when they are with us and will return any which prove unsuitable (provided return postage is supplied), but we cannot take responsibility for the vagaries of the post office, so please retain a photocopy of your manuscript against unfortunate losses.

Select Bibliography

Albert, Michele (aka Michelle Jerott) 2000, *A Great Catch*, Avon Books, New York

——2000, 'Pitching a book', *The Write Touch* newsletter, Wisconsin RWA, <www.michelealbert .com>, April/May 2000

Ashe, Geoffrey 1972, *The Art of Writing Made Simple*, The Chaucer Press, London, p. 147

Atwood, Margaret 1986, 'What is a woman's novel', *Portfolio*, December, p. 96

Banks, Michael A. and Dibell, Ansen 1989, *Word Processing Secrets for Writers*, Writer's Digest Books, Ohio, p. 142

Barnhart, Helen Schellenberg 1983, *Writing Romance for Love and Money*, Writer's Digest Books, Ohio

——1989, 'Turning characters inside out', *Romance Writers Report*, September, pp. 18–20

Bianchi, Jacqui 1984, 'A hero, a heroine and a happy ending', *Moneycare*, National Westminster Bank, London, August, pp. 10–11

Bianchin, Helen 1990, *The Tiger's Lair*, Mills & Boon, London, p. 35

Black, Jaid 2002, *The Empress' New Clothes*, Ellora's Cave, Hudson

Boon, John 1987, 'Romance Not Sex Sells' Mills & Boon', *The Daily Telegraph*, 14 January 1987

Branden, Nathaniel 1981, *The Psychology of Romantic Love*, Bantam, New York

Brown, Sandra 1989, *Long Time Coming*, Loveswept, New York, p. 19

Browning, Dixie 1989, *Beginner's Luck*, Silhouette Desire, New York

Cabot, Heather 2003, 'Chick lit, genre aimed at young women is fueling publishing industry', abcnews.com, New York, 30 August

Calhoon, Charis 2003, 'Harlequin launches single-title inspirational line: Steeple Hill trade paperbacks', *Romance Writers Report,* July, p. 14

Costell, Dianne 2003, 'Up Close and Personal: featuring Valerie Gray of MIRA Books,' *Romance Writers Report*, pp. 44–5

Cole, Bobbie 2003, 'Take a Betty Crocker situation', email, 23 June

Cote, Lyn 2003, 'Market update 2003', *Faith, Hope and Love, the Inspirational Outreach Chapter of RWA,* <www.faithhopelove-rwa.org/markets.htm>

Darcy, Emma 1986, *The Wrong Mirror*, Mills & Boon, London, p. 5

—— 1990, *Bride of Diamonds*, Mills & Boon, London, p. 44

—— 2003, 'Ten Years of the Emma Darcy Award', *Hearts Talk*, March, p. 6

Drew, Jean 2003, 'Preparing for an editorial pitch', *Hearts Talk*, March, p. 3

Edens, Kelly 2003, 'Romance Without the Blush: A look at the inspirational market', Spacecoast Authors of Romance website, <www.authorsofromance.com/inspirational.htm>

Elliott Pickart, Joan 1988, 'Sexual tension puts the "heart" in Golden Heart manuscripts', *Romance Writers*

Report, September. pp. 11–12

Ellora's Cave, 'What is romantica?', <www.ellorascave .com> [2000–2003]

Endlich, Melissa and Marlow Golan, Joan 2003, 'Faith, Love and Beyond', <www.eHarlequin.com>

Farrell, Warren 1986, *Why Men Are the Way They Are*, McGraw-Hill, New York

Faust, Beatrice 1981, *Women, Sex and Pornography*, Penguin Books, Melbourne, pp. 69–70

Fielding, Helen 1996, *Bridget Jones's Diary*, Picador, London

Fielding, Liz 2002, *City Girl in Training,* Harlequin Mills & Boon, p. 14

Freberg, Stan 1976, quoted in *How to Advertise*, St. Martin's Press, New York, p. 40

Garbera, Katherine 2003, 'Making the most of your editor/ agent appointment', <www.katherinegarbera.com>, October

Gisonny, Anne 1981, 'How to write romantic novels', *Romantic Times*, September–October, p. 20

——1982 'Writing your first romantic novel', *Romantic Times*, January–February, p. 15

——1982 'Creating a hero', *Romantic Times*, Holiday, p. 15

Goodyer, Paula 1982, 'Romantic fiction', *Cleo*, July, pp. 32–6

Grenville, Kate 1985, *Lilian's Story*, Allen & Unwin, Sydney

Hager, Jean 1988, 'Beginning greatly', *Romance Writers Report*, March, pp. 12–13

Hannah, Kristin 1996, 'Magic, Myth and Metaphysics: Exploding the Boundaries of Romance', *Romance Writer's Sourcebook,* Writer's Digest Books, Ohio, pp. 48–54

Harlequin Mills & Boon 2003, *Frequently Asked Editorial*

Questions, Handout RWA Conference, Gold Coast

Harris, Thomas 1970, *I'm OK, You're OK*, Pan Books, London

Hudacsek, Ellie 1988, 'Character psychology', *Romance Writers Report*, January, p. 45

Jaffrey, Zareen 2003, 'Deconstructing Bridget Jones', *On Writing Romance*, <www.eHarlequin.com>

James, Melissa 2002, *Her Galahad*, Silhouette Books, New York

Jordan, Penny 1986, *Loving*, Mills & Boon, London, p. 54

Kisha 1979, *Fun With the Stars*, Judicator Publications, Canberra, pp. 29–31

Koop, Rosie 2003, 'Red Dress Ink, the wow factor', speech to Romance Writers of Australia annual conference, Broadbeach, Qld, August

Krentz, Jayne Ann 1992, 'Trying to Tame the Romance', *Dangerous Men and Adventurous Women*, Krentz, Jayne Ann, editor, University of Pennsylvania Press, Philadelphia, p. 112

Lewis, David 1987, *In and Out of Love*, Methuen, London, p. 69

Lovelace, Merline 1994, *Somewhere in Time*, Harlequin Mills & Boon, New York

Lowery, Maralyn M. 1983, *How to Write Romance Novels that Sell*, Rawson Associates, Pennsylvania

Macro, Lucia 1988, 'What makes category romance romantic', *Romance Writers Report*, November, pp. 20–1

McAllister, Anne 1999, *The Playboy and the Nanny*, Harlequin Mills & Boon, London

McCullough, Colleen 1977, *The Thorn Birds*, Harper & Row, New York

McManus, Yvonne 1983, *You Can Write a Romance and Get It Published*, Coronet, New York

Mather, Anne 1974, *Leopard in the Snow*, Mills & Boon, London

Maxwell, Ann 1988, 'And no sagging middles', *Romance Writers Report*, March, p. 21

Mills & Boon 1986, *And Then He Kissed Her . . .*, audio-cassette, London

Mitchell, Margaret 1936, *Gone With the Wind*, Macmillan, London

Napier, Susan 1989, *Another Time*, Harlequin Mills & Boon, London, p. 5, p. 81

Norwood, Robin 1986, *Women Who Love Too Much*, Arrow, London

Novak, Brenda 2003, 'Single title vs series romance: What's the difference?' *On Writing Romance*, <www.eHarlequin.com>

Oxford Dictionary for Writers and Editors, The 1981, Clarendon Press, Oxford

Parv, Valerie 1982, *Love's Greatest Gamble*, Mills & Boon, London

—— 1983, *Remember Me, My Love*, Mills & Boon, London

—— 1983, *The Tall, Dark Stranger*, Mills & Boon, London

—— 1984, *Man and Wife*, Mills & Boon, London

—— 1985, *Ask Me No Questions*, Mills & Boon, London

—— 1985, *Heartbreak Plains*, Mills & Boon, London

—— 1985, *Inherit the Storm*, Mills & Boon, London

—— 1986, *Boss of Yarrakina*, Mills & Boon, London

—— 1986, *Return to Faraway*, Mills & Boon, London

—— 1986, *The Love Artist*, Mills & Boon, London

—— 1987, *Man Shy*, Mills & Boon, London

—— 1987, *Sapphire Nights*, Mills & Boon, London

—— 1987, *Snowy River Man*, Mills & Boon, London

—— 1987, *The Leopard Tree*, Silhouette Books, New York

—— 1988, *Centrefold*, Mills & Boon, London

—— 1988, *Man Without a Past*, Mills & Boon, London

—— 1989, *Tasmanian Devil*, Mills & Boon, London

—— 1990, *That Midas Man*, Mills & Boon, London

—— 1991, *A Fair Exchange*, Mills & Boon, London

—— 1995, *The Idea Factory*, Allen & Unwin, Sydney

—— 2000, *The Monarch's Son*, Silhouette Romances, New York

—— 2001, *Booties and the Beast*, Silhouette Romances, New York

—— 2001, *Interrupted Lullaby*, Silhouette Intimate Moments, New York

—— 2002, *Royal Spy*, Silhouette Intimate Moments, New York

—— 2002, *The Baron and the Bodyguard*, Silhouette Romances, New York

—— 2003, *Operation Monarch*, Silhouette Intimate Moments, New York

—— 2003, *The Prince and the Marriage Pact*, Silhouette Romances, New York

—— 2004, *Heir to Danger*, Silhouette Intimate Moments, New York

Pocket Oxford Dictionary 1969, Oxford University Press, London

Pournelle, Jerry 1976, 'The construction of believable societies', in *The Craft of Science Fiction*, Brettnor, Harper & Row, New York, p. 117

Provost, Gary 1980, *Make Every Word Count*, Writer's Digest Books, Ohio, p. 151

Richard-Akers, Nancy 1988, 'The magic ingredient', *Romance Writers Report*, November, p. 19

Roberts, Nora 1999, *The Donovan Legacy*, Harlequin Mills & Boon, New York

Roddenberry, Gene 1984, *The Literary View of the Future*,

audiocassette, World Future Society, Washington DC

Roe, Paula 2003, 'Our Emma Darcy Award winners—where are they now?', *Hearts Talk*, April, pp. 8–9

'RWA's 2003 RITA and Golden Heart Contests' 2002, Romance Writers of America, *Romance Writers Report* vol. 22, no. 10, pp. 32–8

Seger, Linda 1987, *Making a Good Script Great*, Dodd, Mead & Company, New York, p. 118

Sorrels, Roy 1985, 'Real men don't quirk: Creating a believably romantic couple', *Fiction Writers Monthly*, no. 14, September, pp. 6–8

Starratt, Tanya Saari 2003, 'Talking with Tanya Starratt,' <www.eHarlequin.com>

Style, Linda 2003, 'Pitching your book: 10 tips for a great editor interview', <www.lindastyle.com_ten_tips.html>, October

Taylor Bradford, Barbara 1979, *A Woman of Substance*, Doubleday, New York

Wibberley, Mary 1985, *To Writers With Love*, Buchan & Enright, London

Wright, Daphne 1991, 'Crime versus romance', *Million*, London, November–December, pp. 33–5

Index